A Step by Step Guide
CogAT – Form 7
(Cognitive Abilities Test)

NUMBER
SERIES

Grade 2
By MindMine

CONCEPT:

Based on the pattern, find what goes on the line with the question mark?

STEP-1: Count number of circles on each line

STEP-2: Analyze the pattern

Note: A line with NO circles should be counted as ZERO

STEP-3: Find the answer based on the pattern

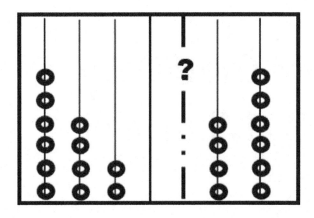

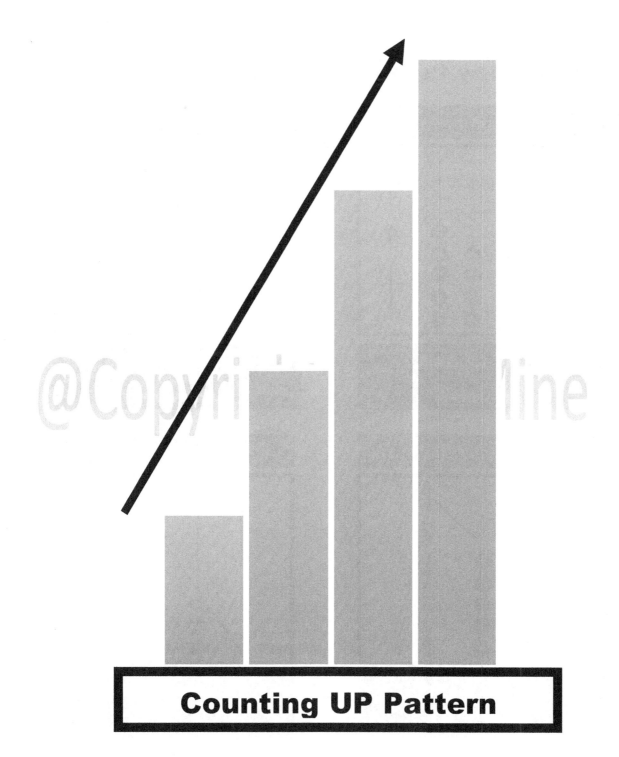

Counting UP Pattern

Count UP: by 1's or 2's or 3's etc.,

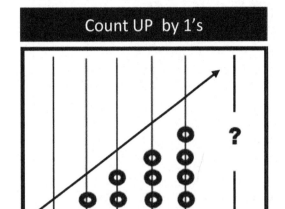

Count UP by 1's

Pattern 1,2,3,4,5,?

Answer=6

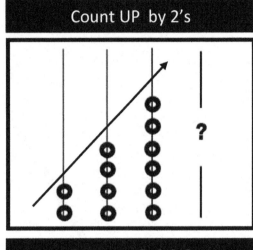

Count UP by 2's

Pattern 2,4,6,?

Answer=8

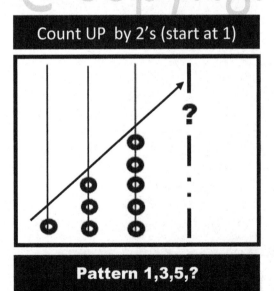

Count UP by 2's (start at 1)

Pattern 1,3,5,?

Answer=7

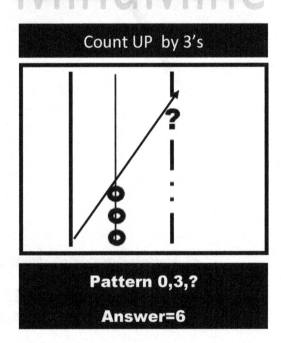

Count UP by 3's

Pattern 0,3,?

Answer=6

1

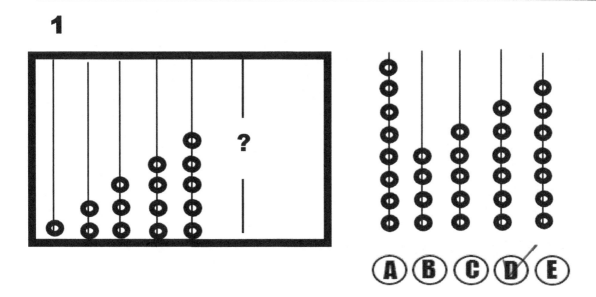

2

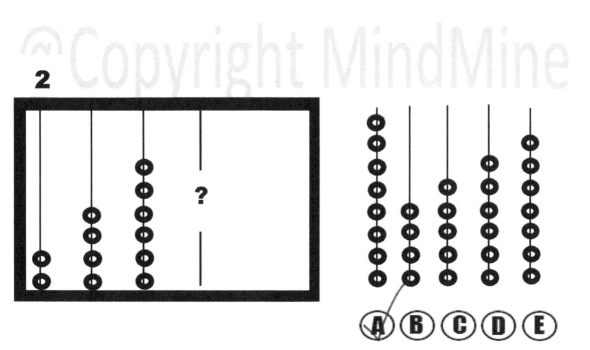

3

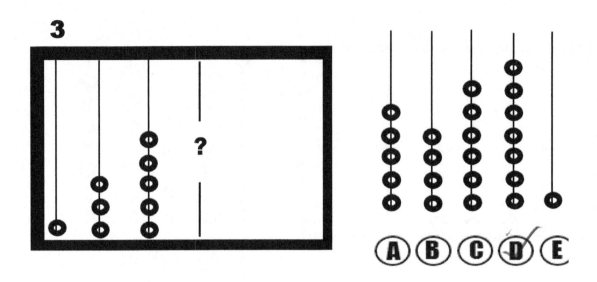

4

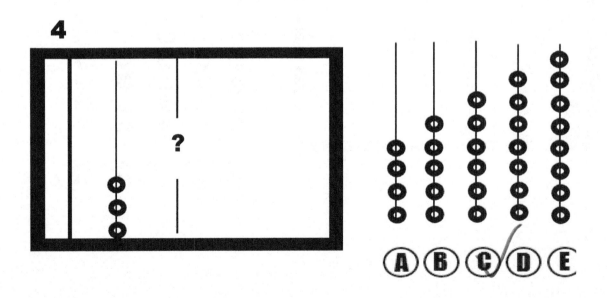

5

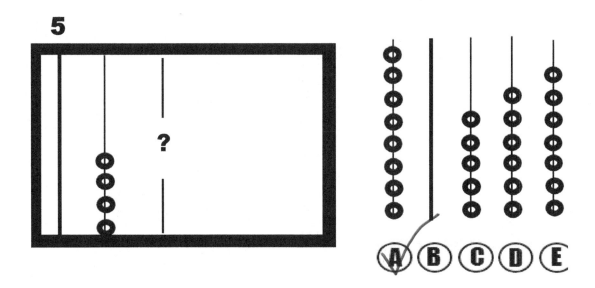

6

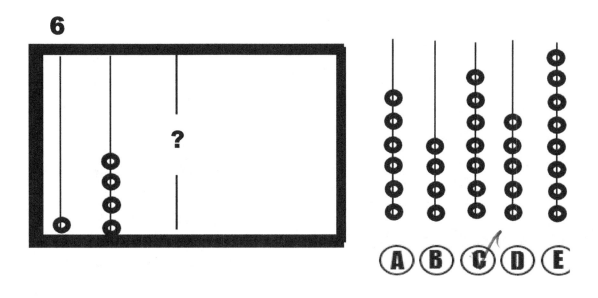

7

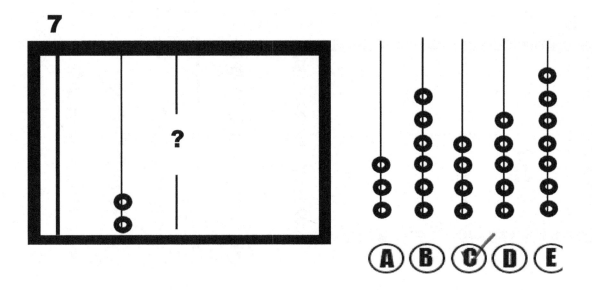

8

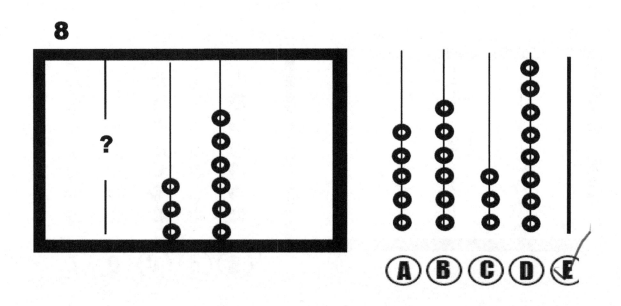

9

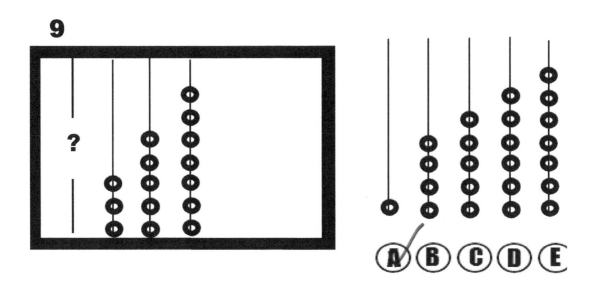

10

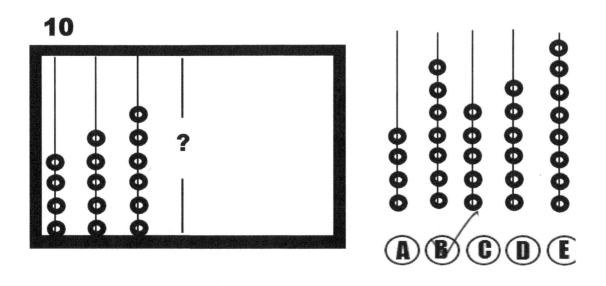

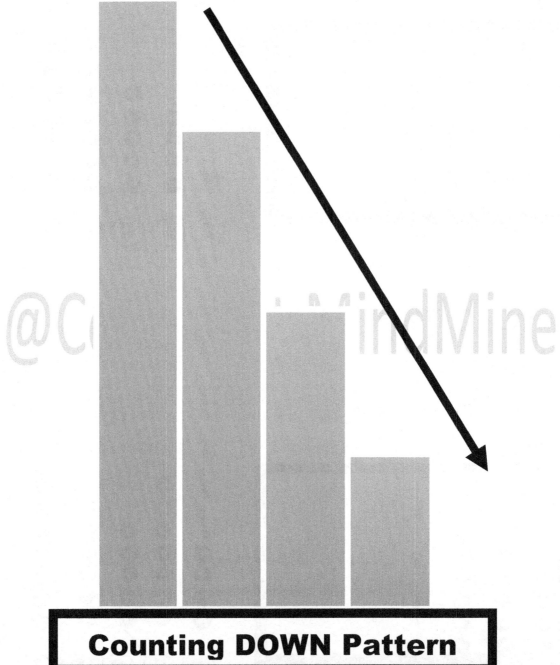

Counting DOWN Pattern

Count DOWN: by 1's or 2's or 3's etc.,

Count DOWN by 1's

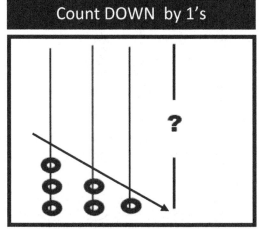

Pattern 3,2,1,?

Answer=0

Count DOWN by 4's

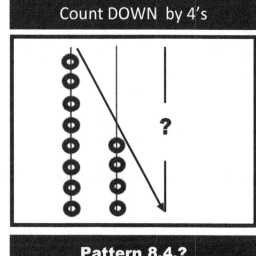

Pattern 8,4,?

Answer=0

Count DOWN by 2's

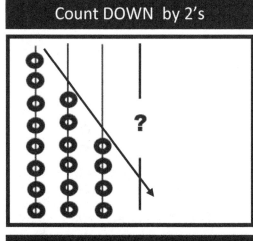

Pattern 8,6,4,?

Answer=2

Count DOWN by 3's

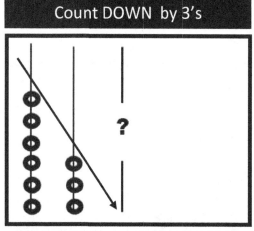

Pattern 6,3,?

Answer=0

1

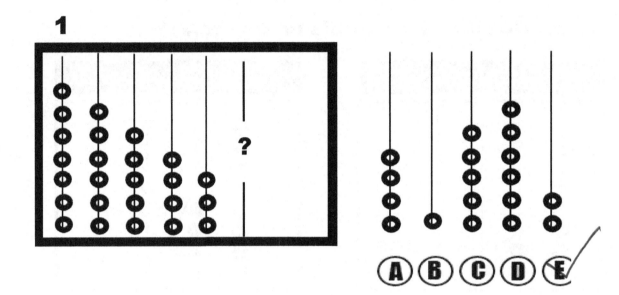

2

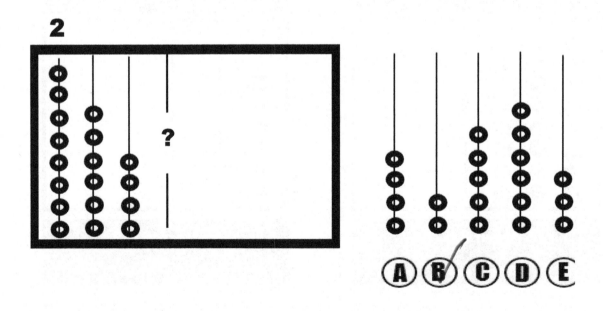

3

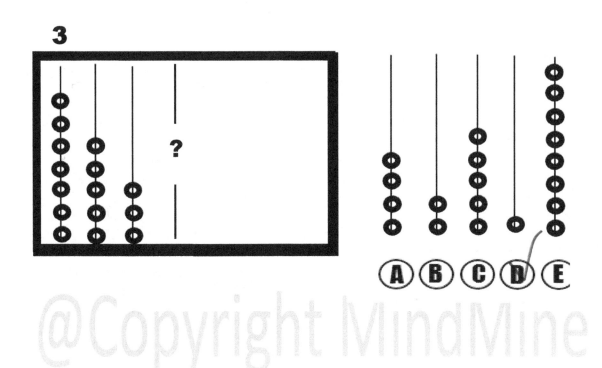

4

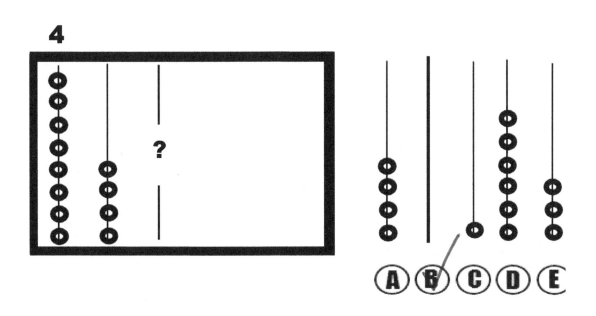

5

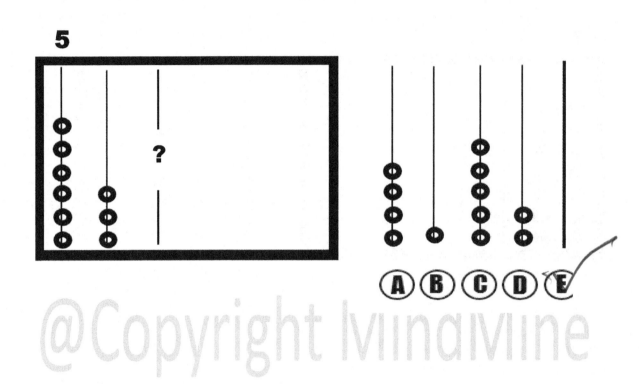

6

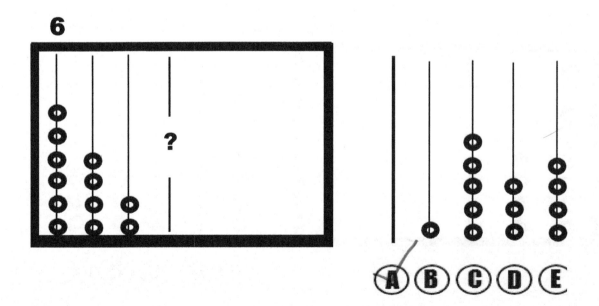

7

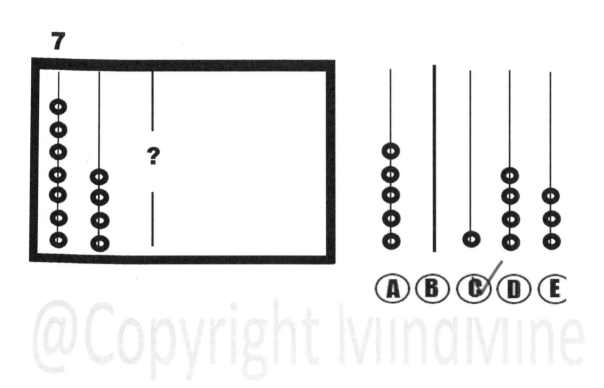

8

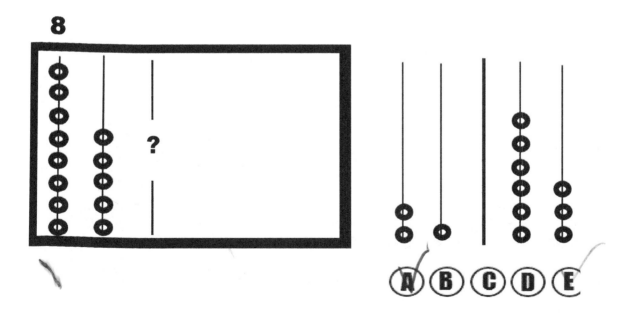

9

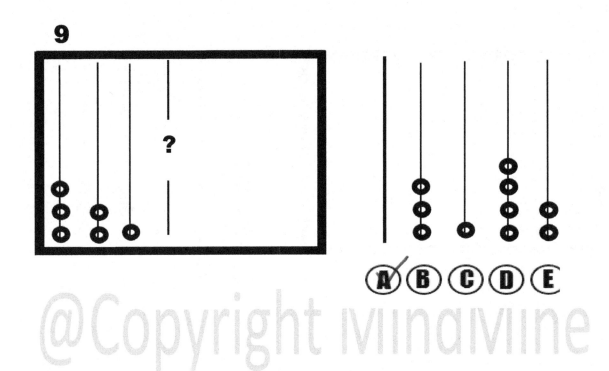

10

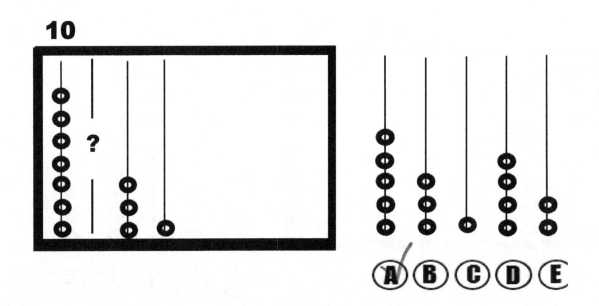

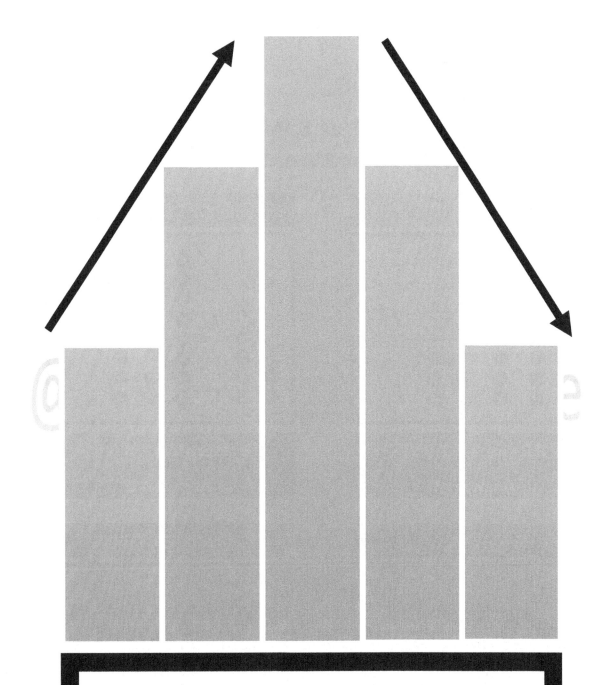

Counting UP then DOWN Pattern

Count UP then DOWN: by 1's or 2's or 3's etc.,

[OR]

Count UP then START at Same Number and Count DOWN: by 1's or 2's or 3's etc.,

Count UP-DOWN by 2's

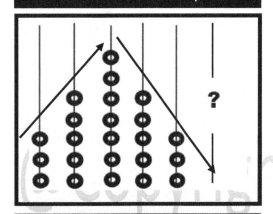

Pattern 3,5,7,5,3?

Answer=1

Count UP-DOWN by 2's

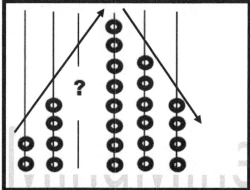

Pattern 2,4,?,8,6,4

Answer=6

Count UP-STAY-DOWN by 2's

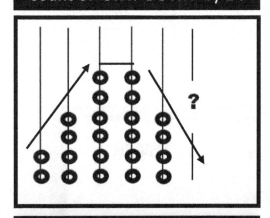

Pattern 2,4,6,6,?

Answer=2

Count UP-DOWN by 3's

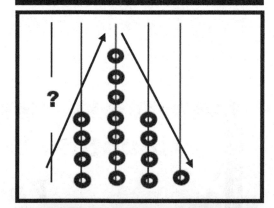

Pattern ?,4,7,4,1

Answer=1

1

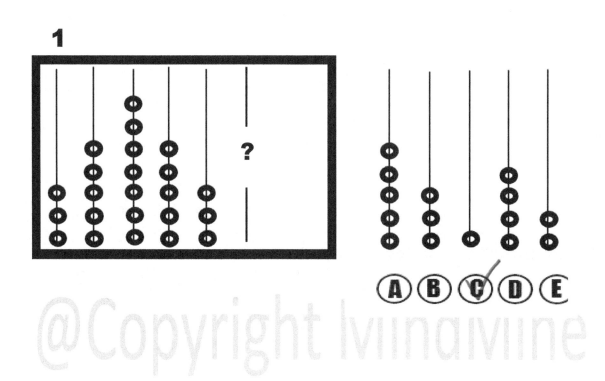

2

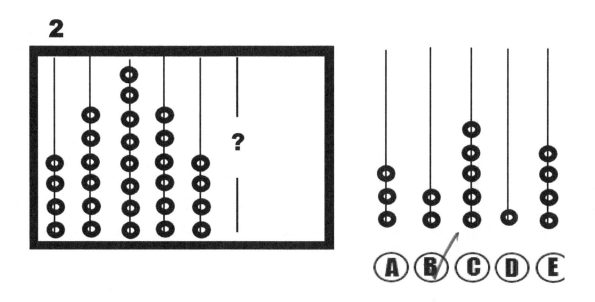

3

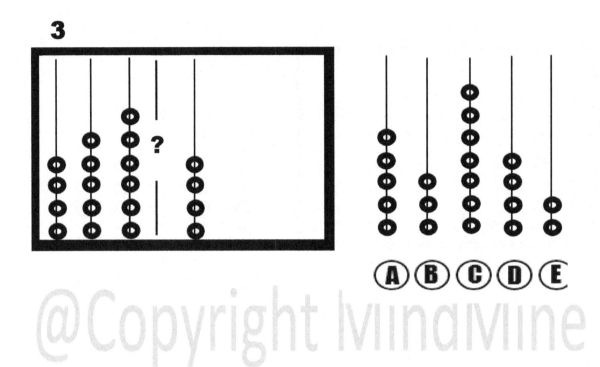

4

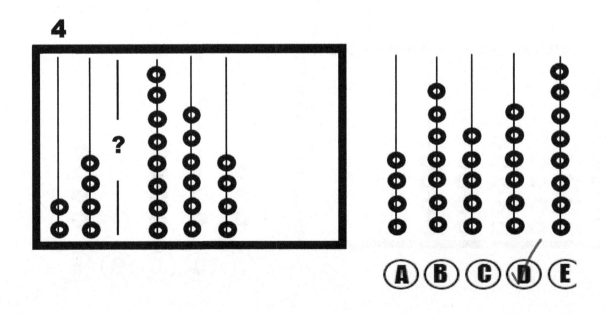

5

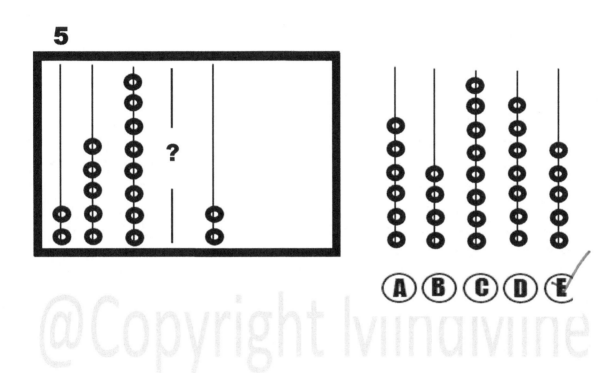

6

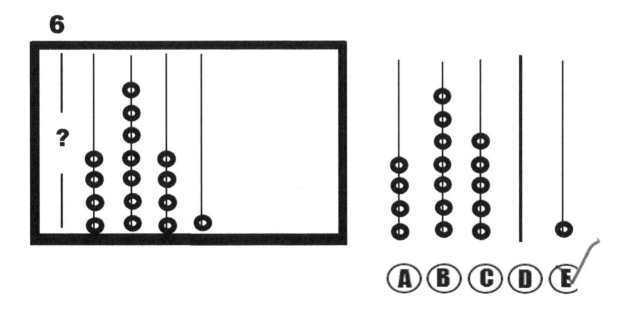

7

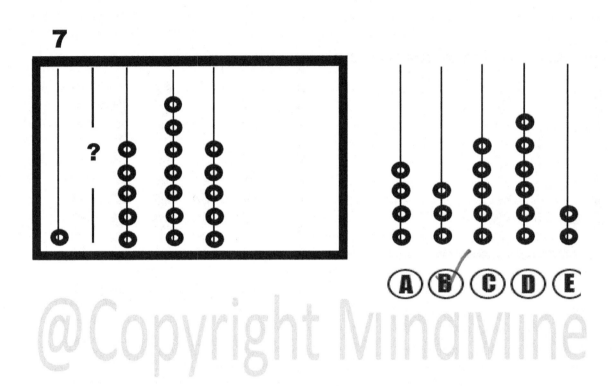

8

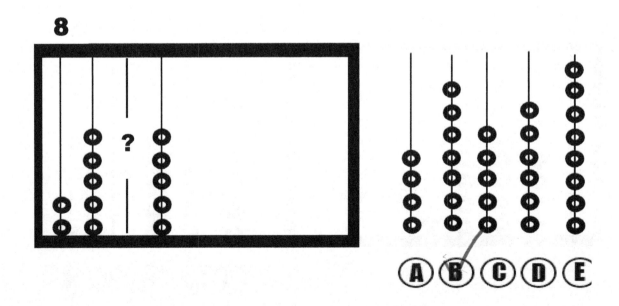

9

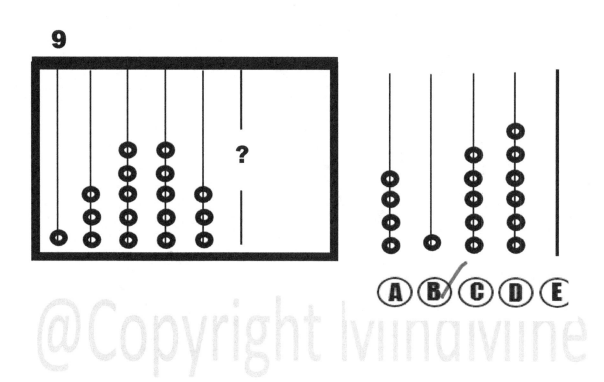

10

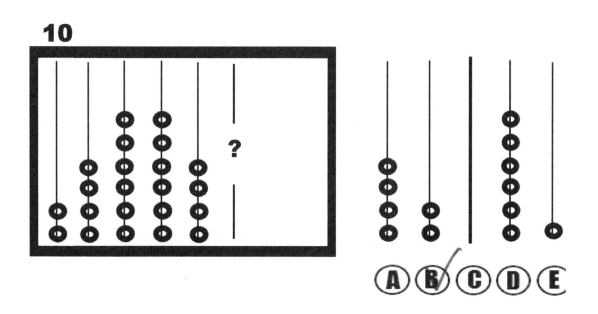

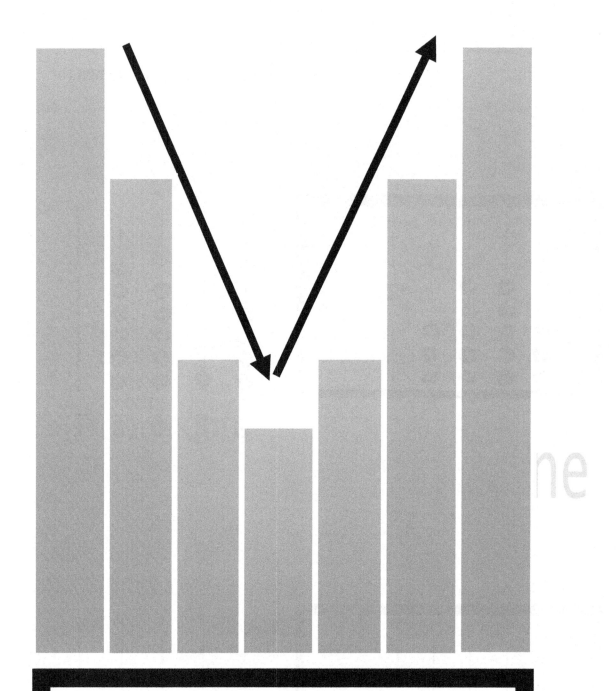

Counting DOWN then UP Pattern

Count DOWN then UP: by 1's or 2's or 3's etc.,

[OR]

Count DOWN then START at Same Number and Count UP: by 1's or 2's or 3's etc.,

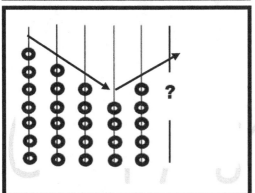

Count DOWN-UP by 1's

Pattern 7,6,5,4,5,?

Answer=6

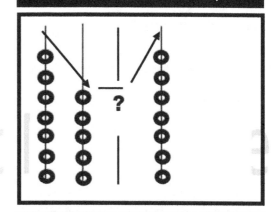

Count DOWN-STAY-UP by 2's

Pattern 7,5,?,7

Answer=5

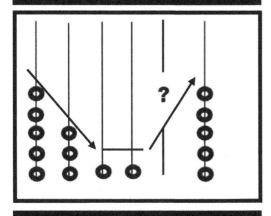

Count DOWN-STAY-UP by 2's

Pattern 5,3,1,1,?,5

Answer=3

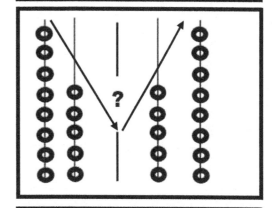

Count UP-DOWN by 3's

Pattern 8,5,?,5,8

Answer=2

1

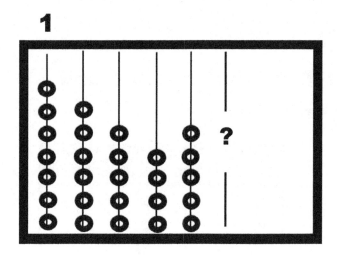

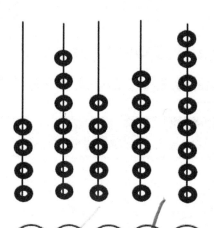

2

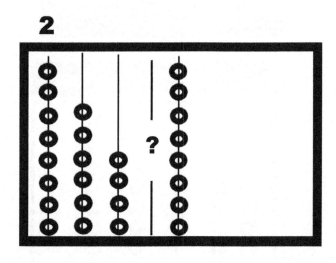

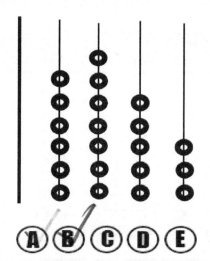

3

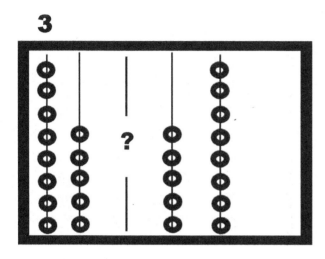

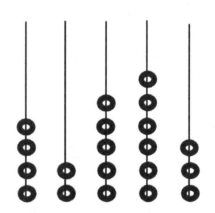

Ⓐ Ⓑ Ⓒ Ⓓ Ⓔ

4

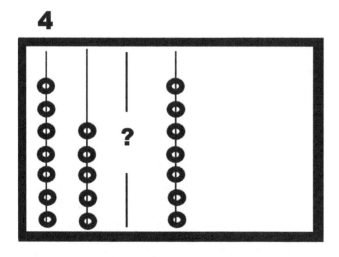

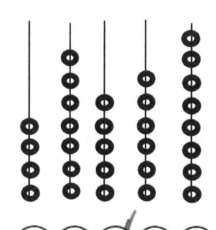

Ⓐ Ⓑ Ⓒ Ⓓ Ⓔ

5

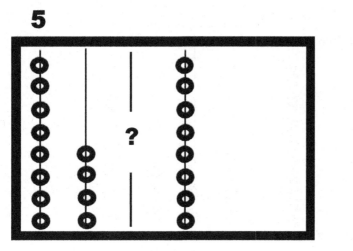

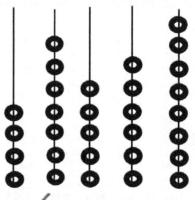

6

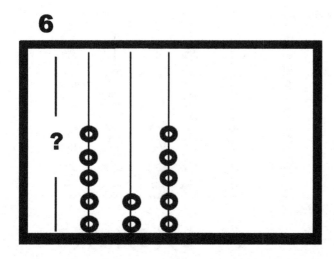

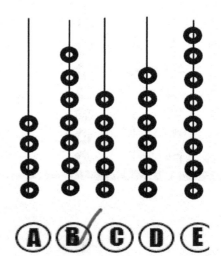

7

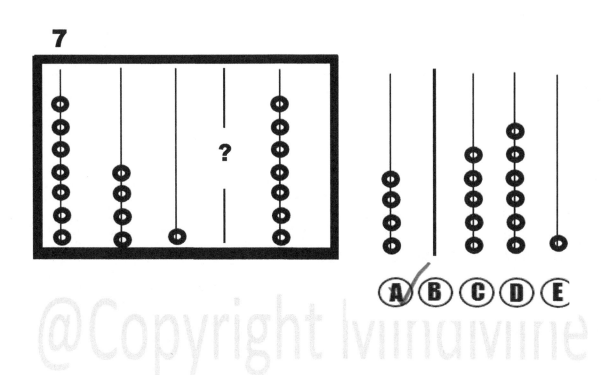

8

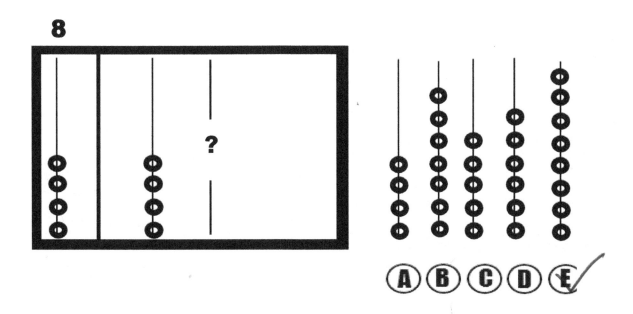

9

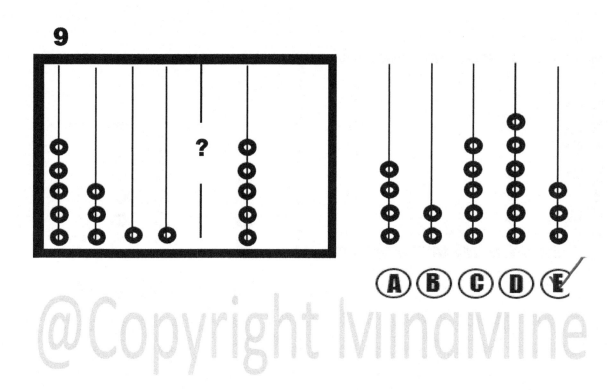

10

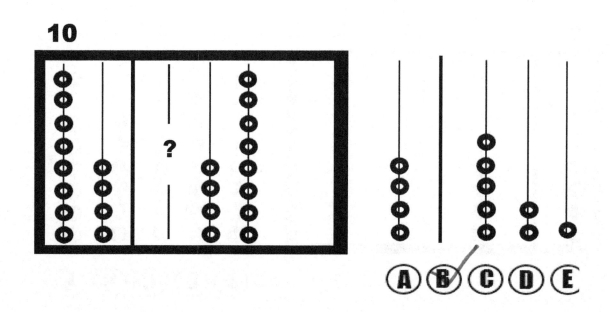

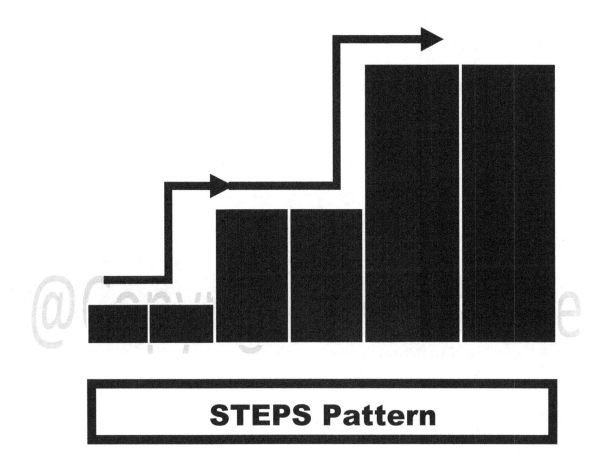

STEPS Pattern

Count: UP or DOWN or UP-DOWN or DOWN-UP.
Repeat a number twice or thrice

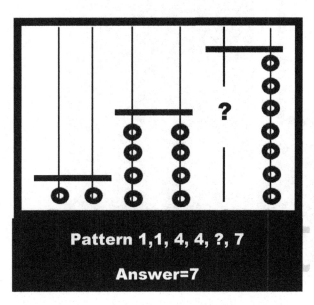

Pattern 1,1, 4, 4, ?, 7

Answer=7

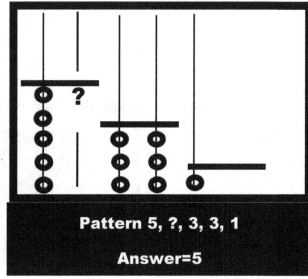

Pattern 5, ?, 3, 3, 1

Answer=5

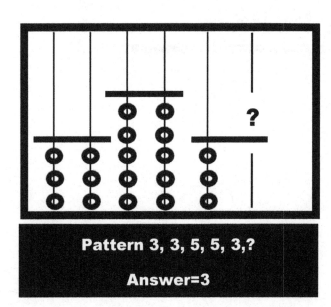

Pattern 3, 3, 5, 5, 3,?

Answer=3

1

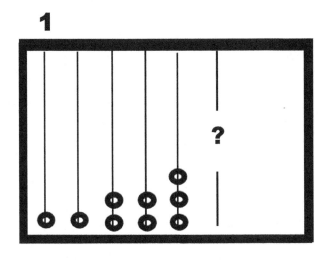

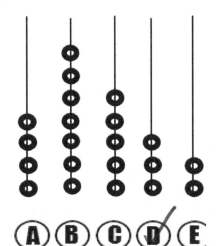

2

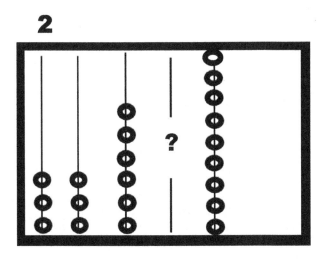

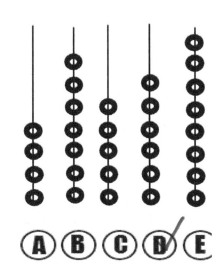

3

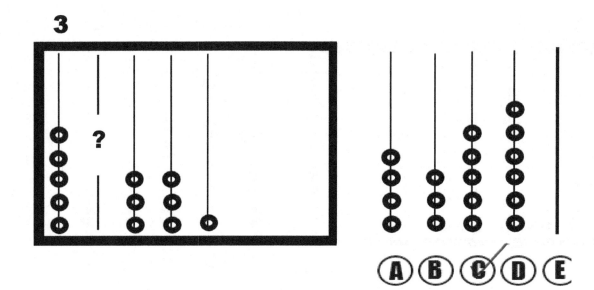

4

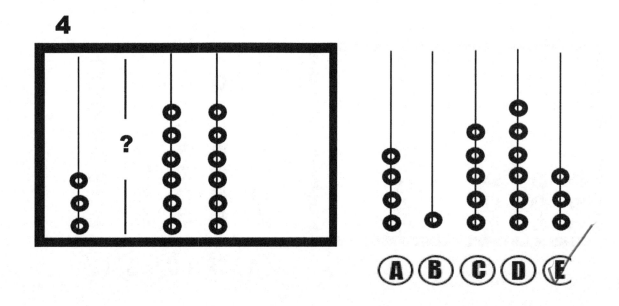

5

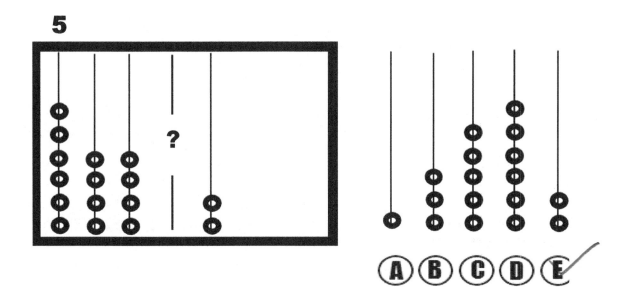

6

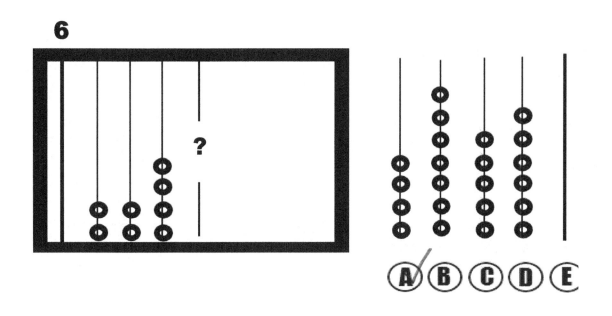

7

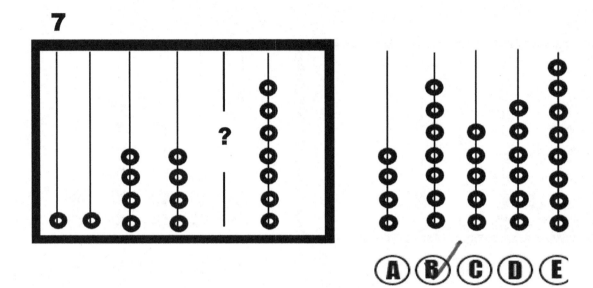

8

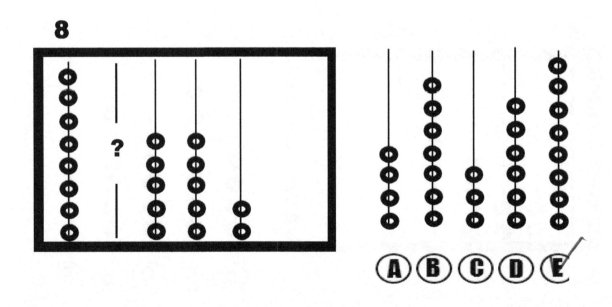

9

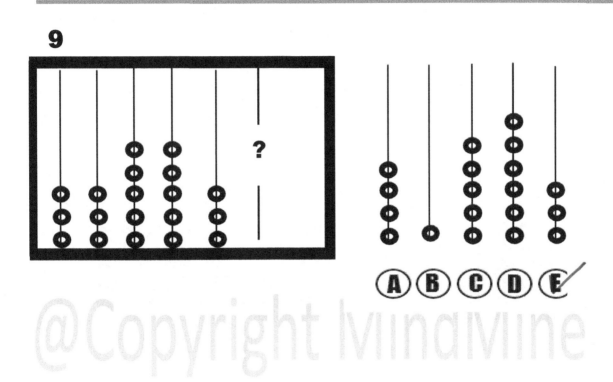

10

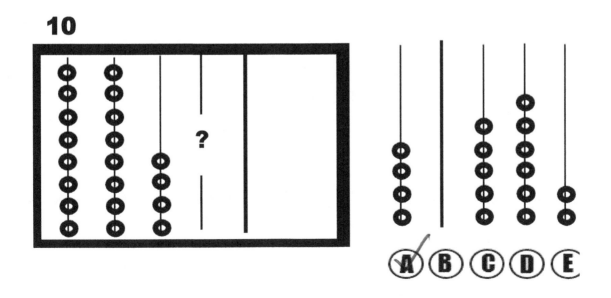

AB Pattern

CONCEPT: Repetition of TWO Numbers

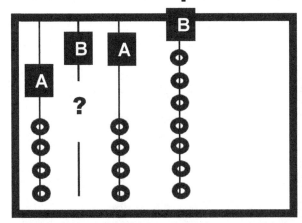

Pattern 4,?,4,7

Answer=7

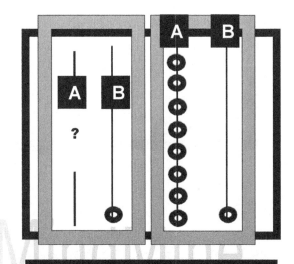

Pattern ?,1,8,1

Answer=8

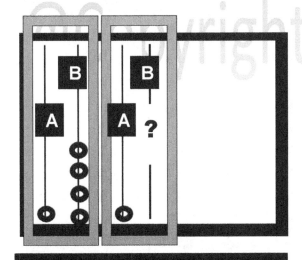

Pattern 1,4,1,?

Answer=4

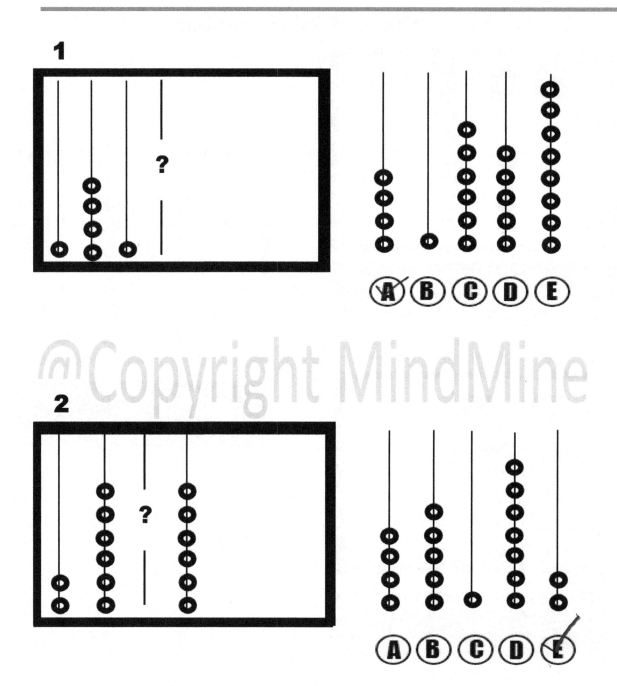

3

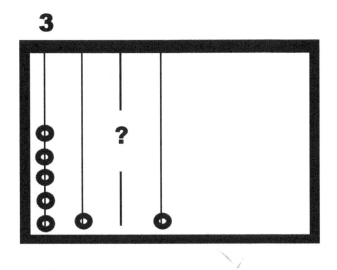

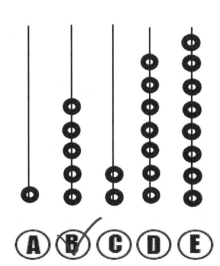

Ⓐ Ⓑ Ⓒ Ⓓ Ⓔ

4

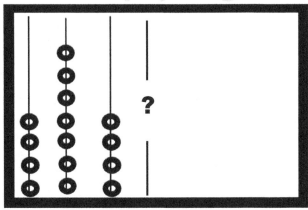

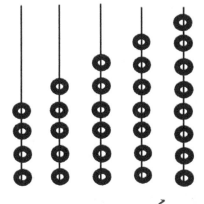

Ⓐ Ⓑ Ⓒ Ⓓ Ⓔ

5

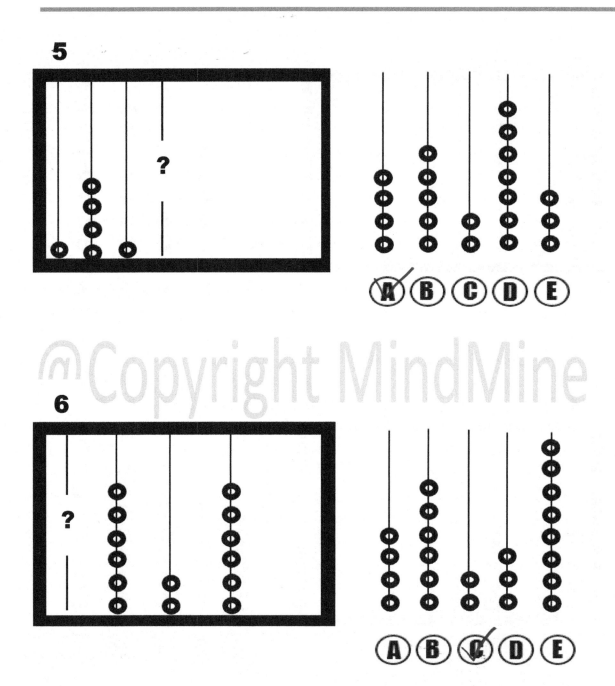

6

7

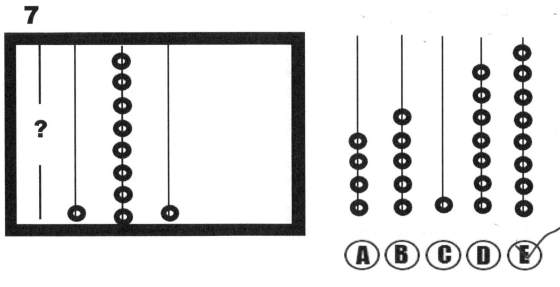

Ⓐ Ⓑ Ⓒ Ⓓ Ⓔ

8

Ⓐ Ⓑ Ⓒ Ⓓ Ⓔ

9

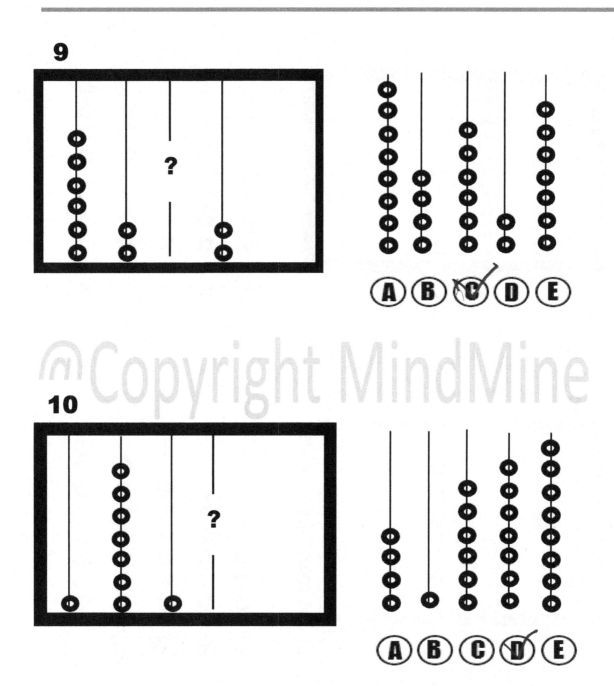

10

11

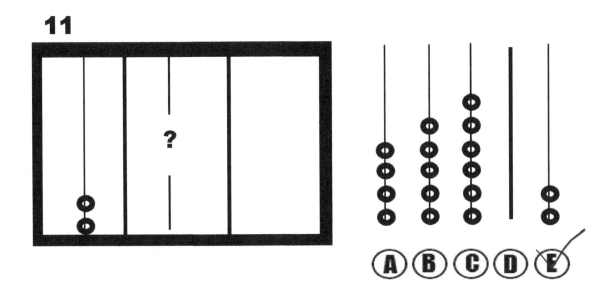

12

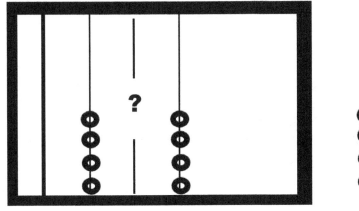

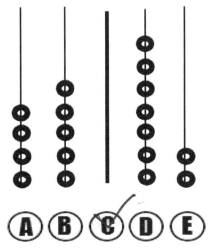

A B C | A B C

ABC Pattern

Concept: Repetition of THREE Numbers

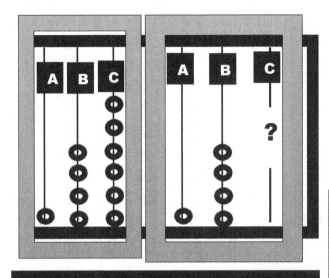

Pattern 1,4,6,1,4,?

Answer=6

Pattern ?,0,6,2,0,6

Answer=2

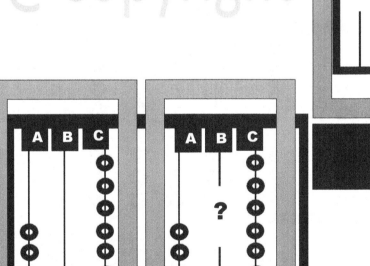

Pattern 4,2,7,4,?,7

Answer=2

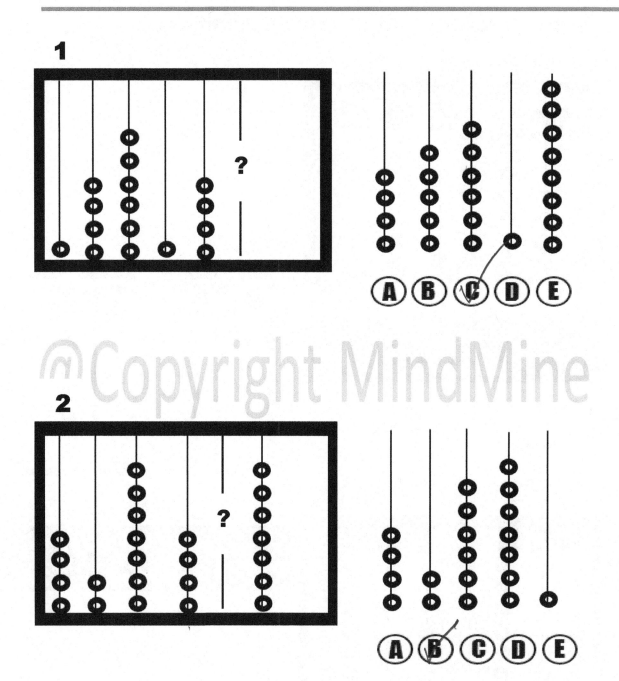

3

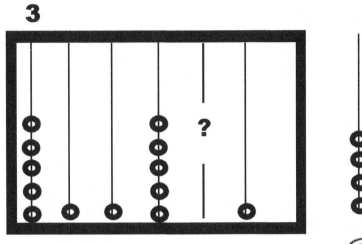

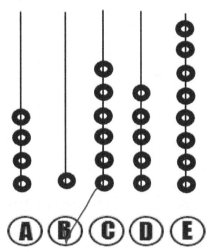

4

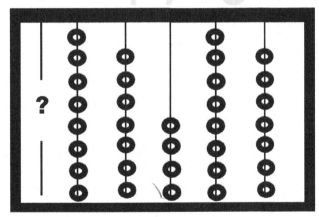

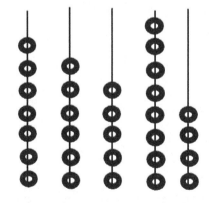

5

6

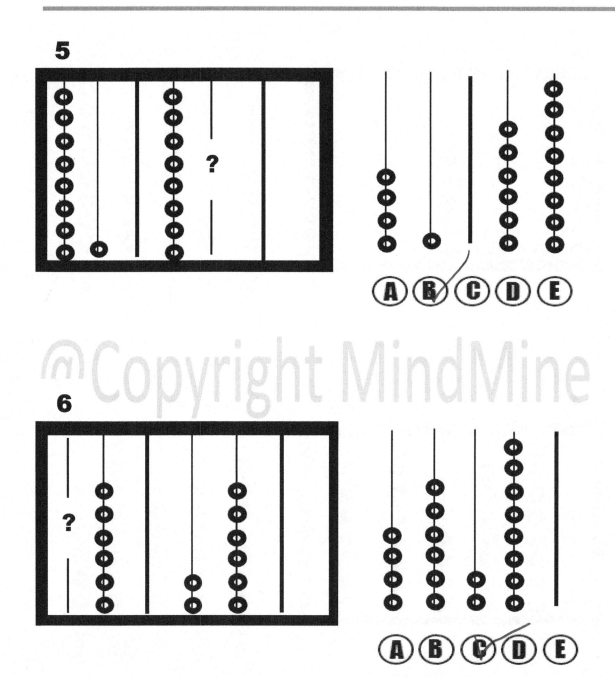

7

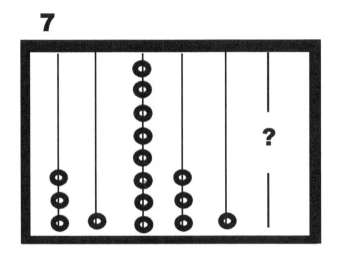

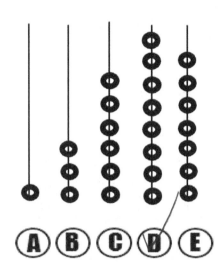

8

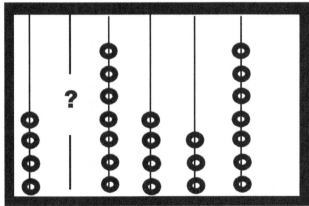

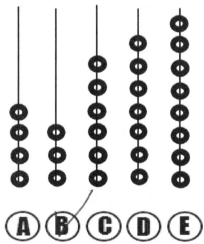

9

10

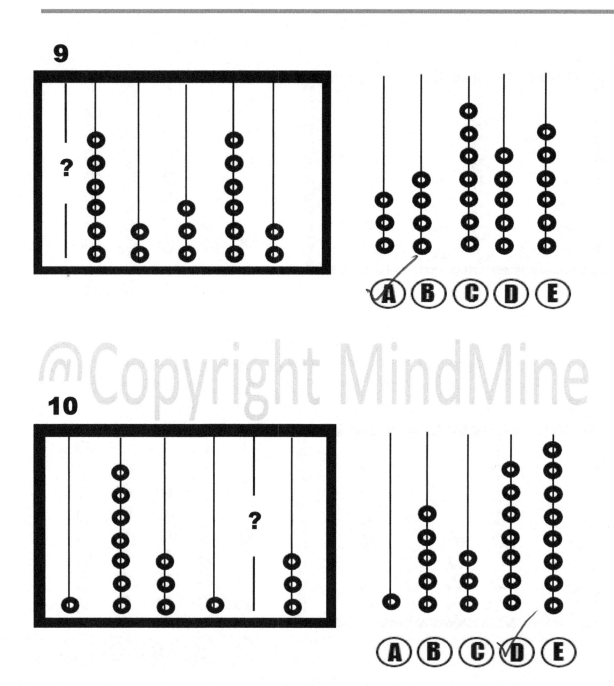

11

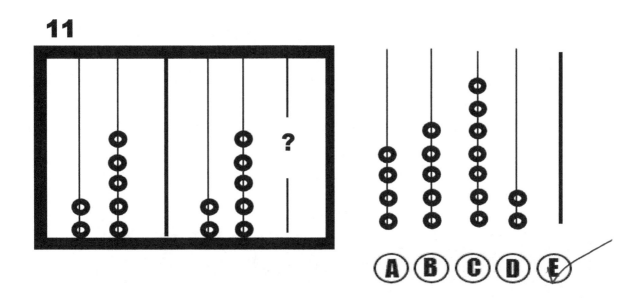

12

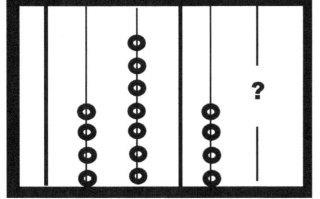

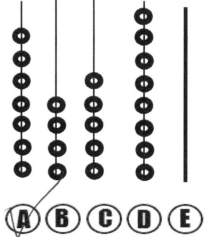

A B C D | A B C D

ABCD Pattern

Concept: Repetition of FOUR Numbers

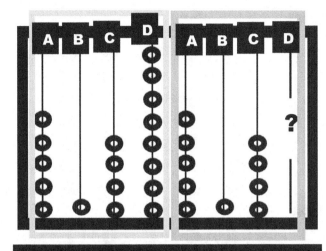

Pattern 5,1,4,8,5,1,4,?

Answer=8

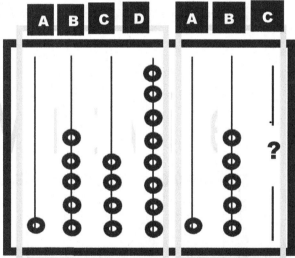

Pattern 1,5,4,8,1,5,?

Answer=4

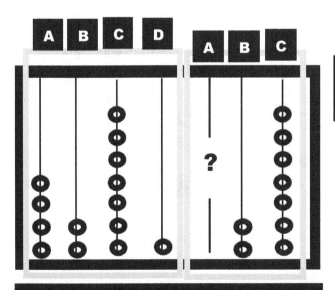

Pattern 4,2,7,1,?,2,7

Answer=4

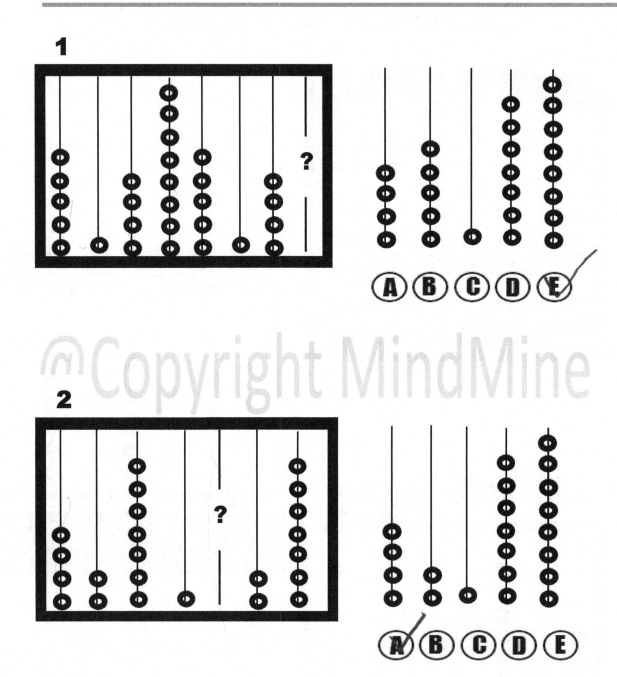

3

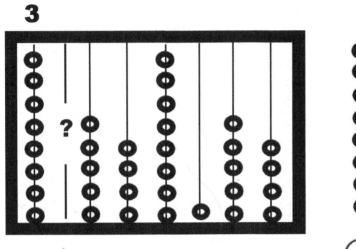 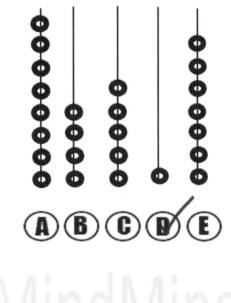

4

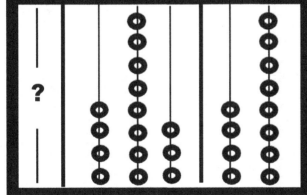 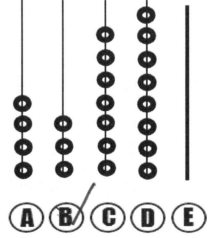

5

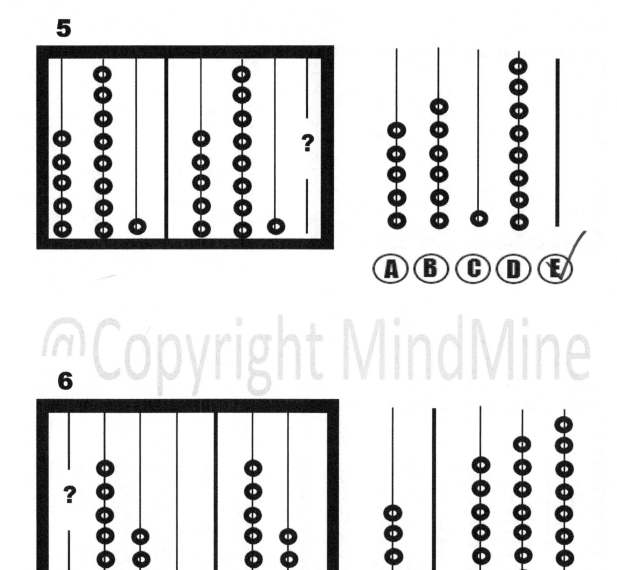

6

7

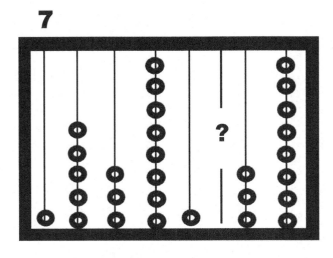

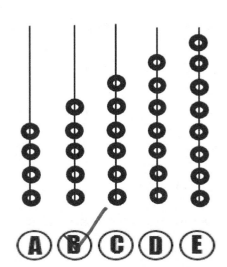

Ⓐ Ⓑ Ⓒ Ⓓ Ⓔ

8

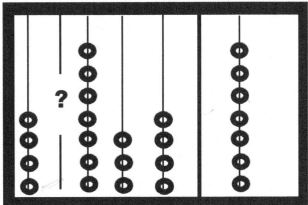

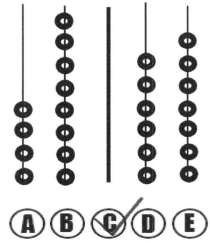

Ⓐ Ⓑ Ⓒ Ⓓ Ⓔ

9

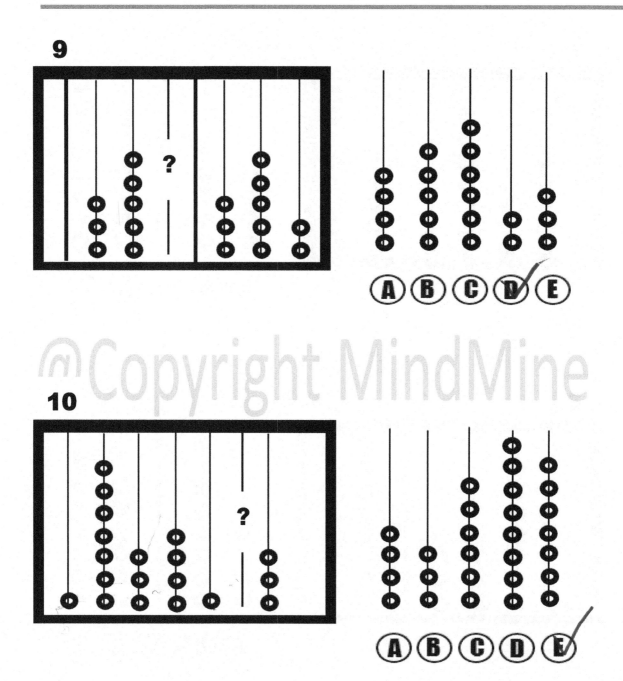

10

11

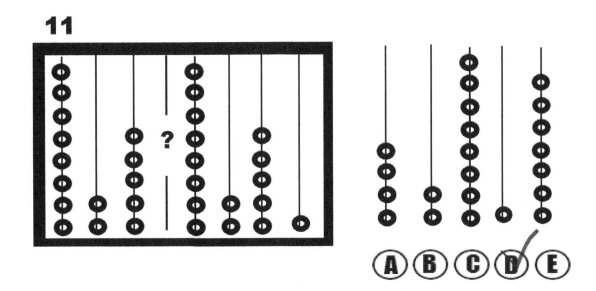

12

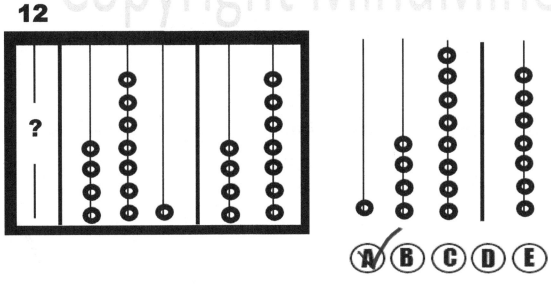

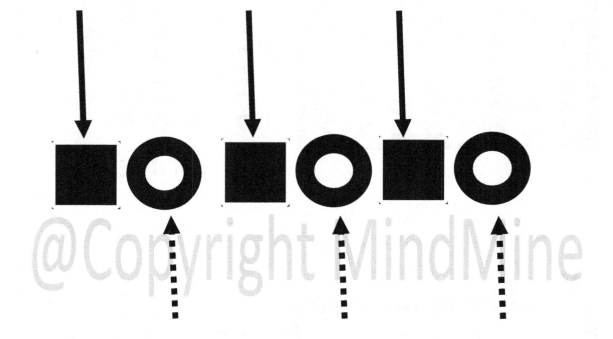

SKIP Pattern

Concept:

Look one, Skip one. Look one, Skip one........

Looked ones are in one Pattern.

Skipped ones are in another Pattern

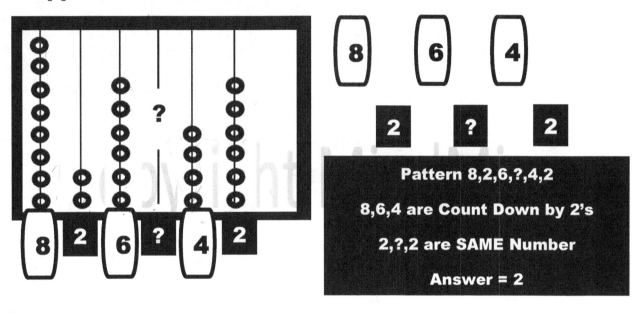

Pattern 8,2,6,?,4,2

8,6,4 are Count Down by 2's

2,?,2 are SAME Number

Answer = 2

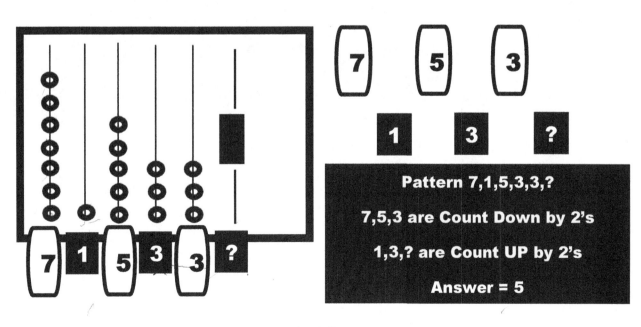

Pattern 7,1,5,3,3,?

7,5,3 are Count Down by 2's

1,3,? are Count UP by 2's

Answer = 5

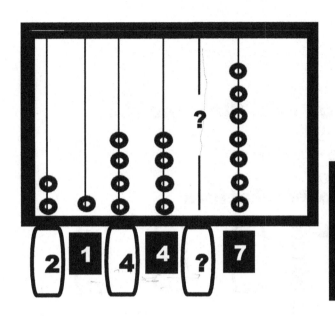

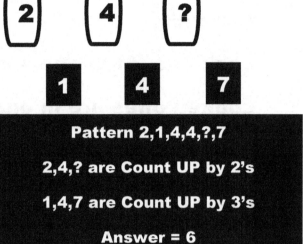

Pattern 2,1,4,4,?,7

2,4,? are Count UP by 2's

1,4,7 are Count UP by 3's

Answer = 6

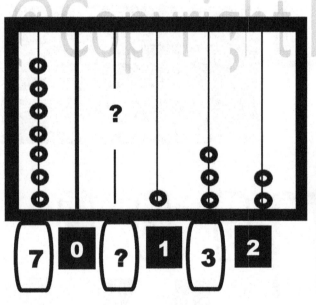

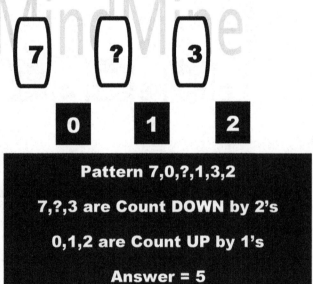

Pattern 7,0,?,1,3,2

7,?,3 are Count DOWN by 2's

0,1,2 are Count UP by 1's

Answer = 5

1

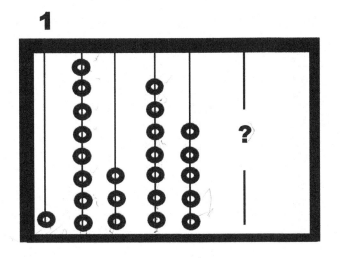
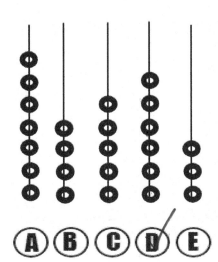

2

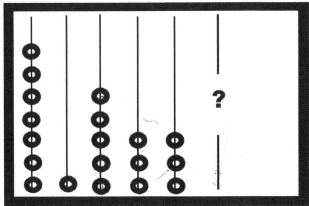
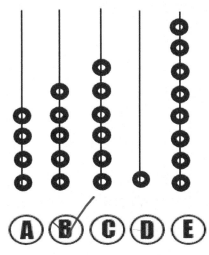

3

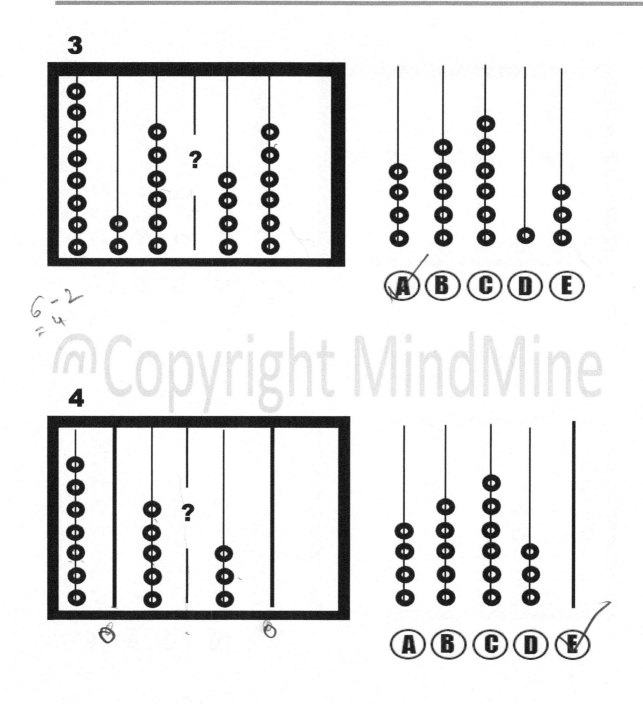

4

5

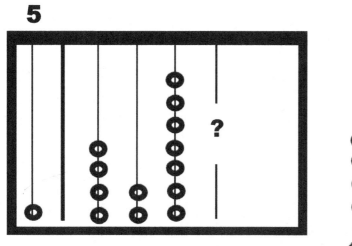

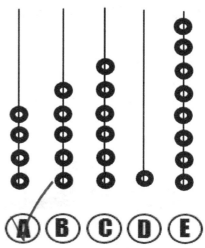

6

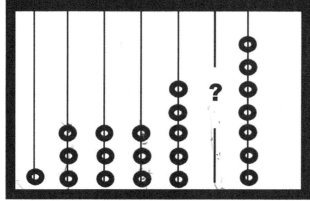

7

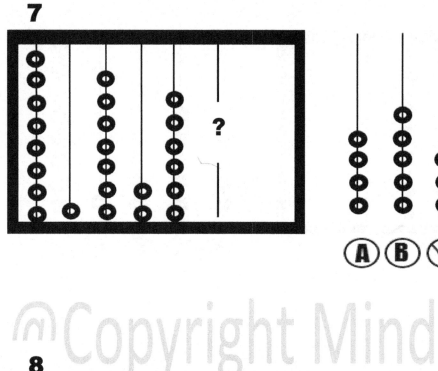

8

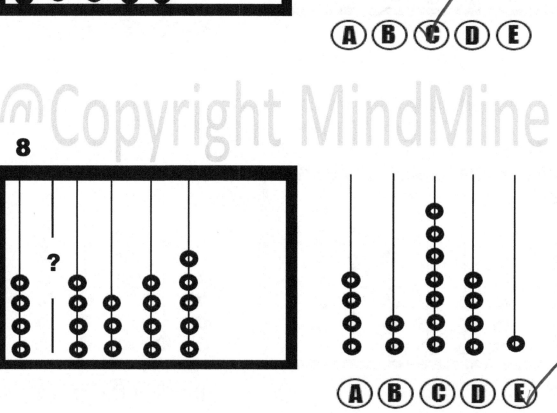

9

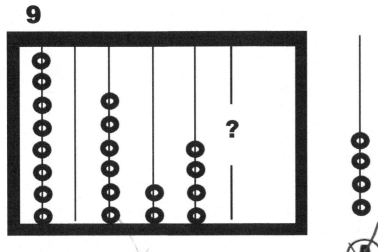

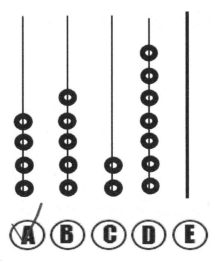

Ⓐ Ⓑ Ⓒ Ⓓ Ⓔ

10

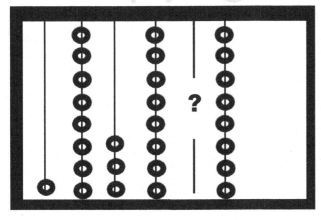

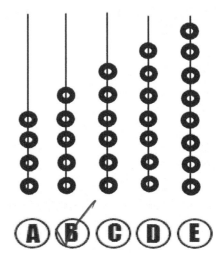

Ⓐ Ⓑ Ⓒ Ⓓ Ⓔ

11

12

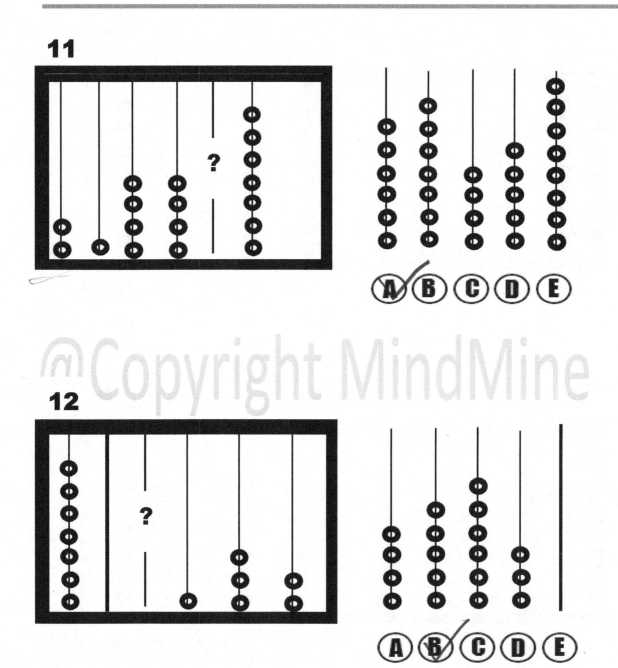

13

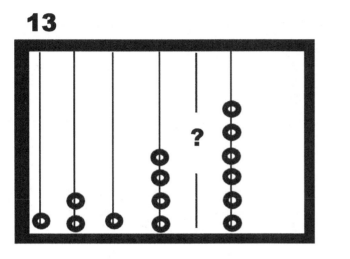

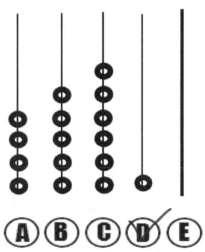

A **B** **C** **D** **E**

14

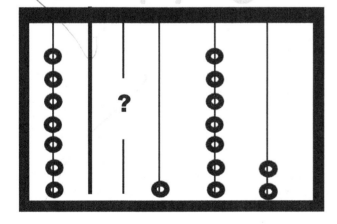

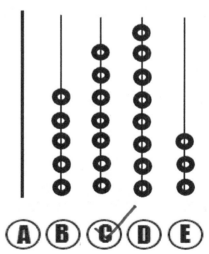

A **B** **C** **D** **E**

15

16

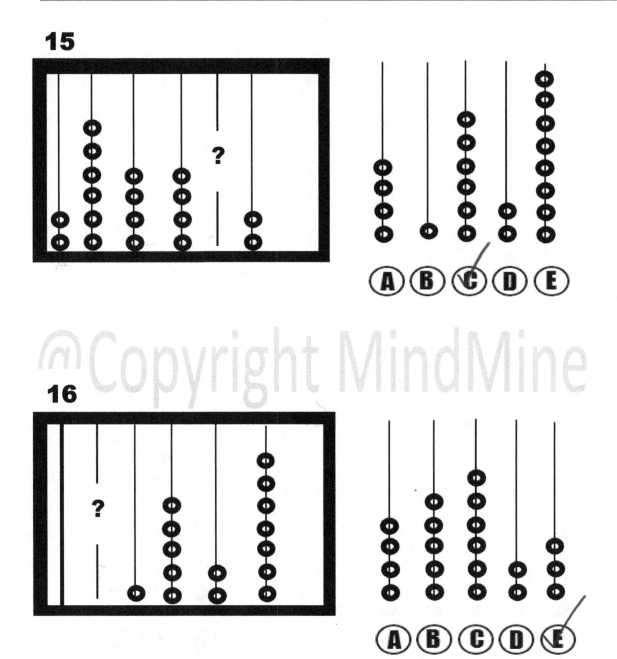

17

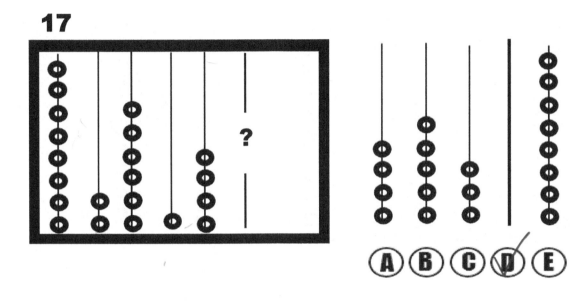

18

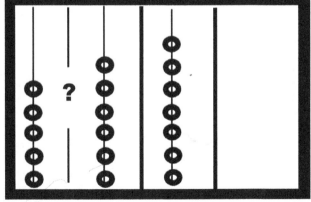

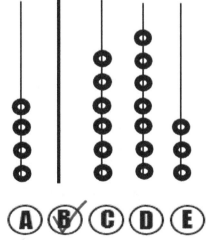

19

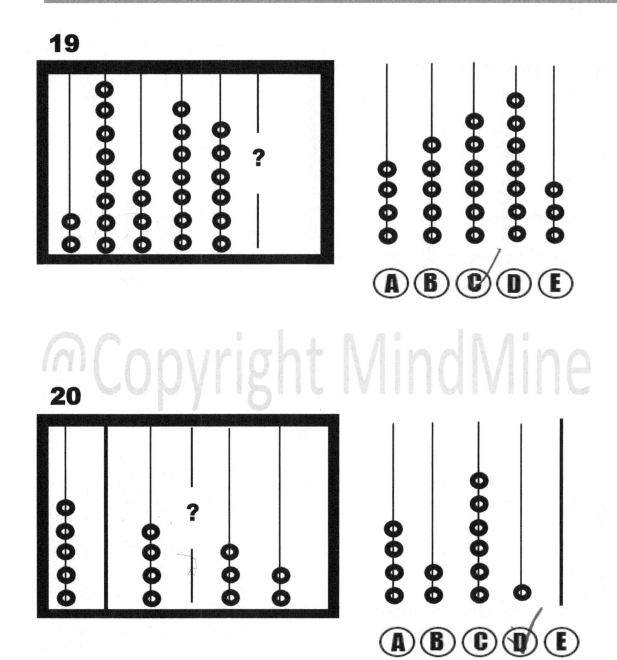

20

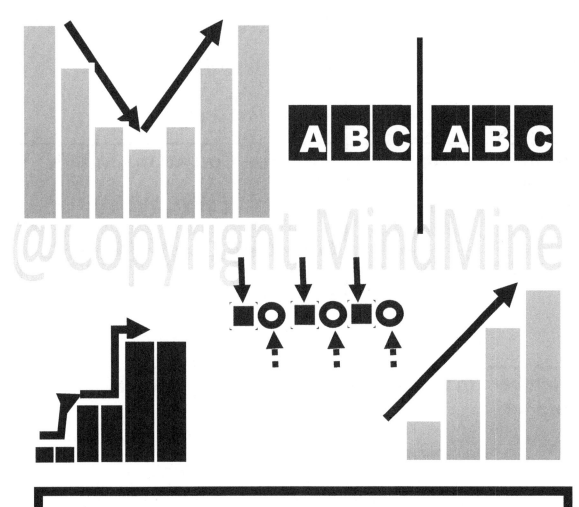

Application of Analytical Skills

Numbers going UP?	Look for Counting UP (or) Counting UP then Down (or) STEPS Pattern
Numbers going DOWN?	Look for Counting DOWN (or) Counting Down then UP (or) STEPS Pattern
Numbers in Random order?	Look for AB Pattern (or) ABC Pattern (or) ABCD Pattern
Numbers in Random order & Not in AB/ABC/ABCD Pattern	Apply SKIP Pattern

1

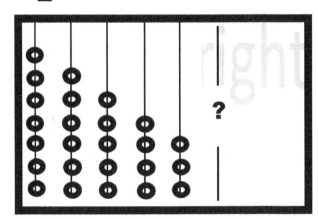

Numbers Going Up? NO

Numbers Going Down? NO

Numbers in random order? YES

AB Pattern? NO

ABC Pattern? YES

Answer = 3

2

Numbers Going Up? NO

Numbers Going Down? YES

Use Counting DOWN Pattern

Answer = 2

3

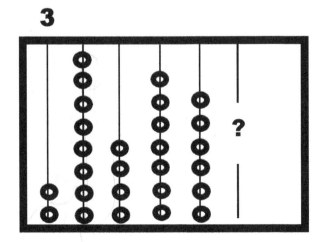

Numbers Going Up? NO

Numbers Going Down? NO

Numbers in random order? YES

AB Pattern? NO

ABC Pattern? NO

ABCD Pattern? NO

Use SKIP Pattern

Answer = 6

4

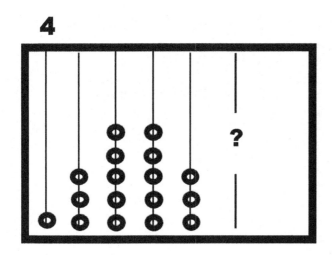

Numbers Going Up? Yes

Use Counting Up then Down Pattern

Answer = 1

5

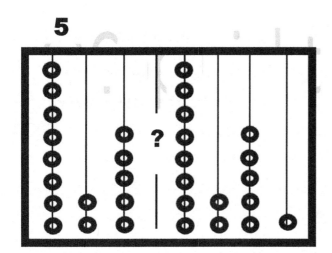

Numbers Going Up? NO

Numbers Going Down? NO

Numbers in random order? YES

AB Pattern? NO

ABC Pattern? NO

ABCD Pattern? YES

Answer = 1

6

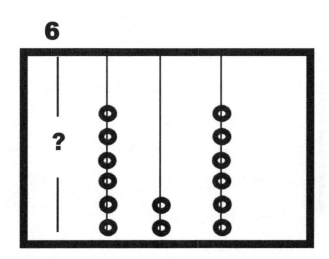

Numbers Going Up? NO

Numbers Going Down? YES

Counting Down then up? YES

Answer = 8

Note: It could be AB Pattern

Answer = 2

Pick 8 or 2 from given answer choices (You will see only one answer choice either 8 or 2)

7

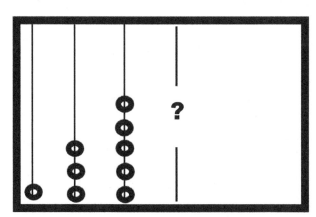

Numbers Going Up? Yes

Answer = 7

8

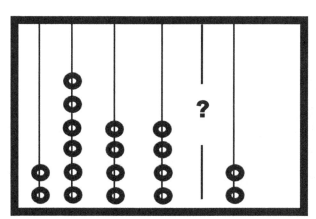

Numbers Going Up? NO

Numbers Going Down? NO

Numbers in random order? YES

AB Pattern? NO

ABC Pattern? NO

ABCD Pattern? NO

Use SKIP Pattern

Answer = 6

9

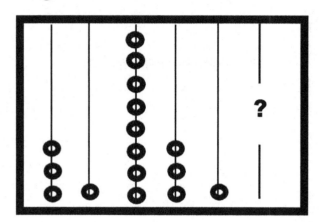

Numbers Going Up? NO

Numbers Going Down? NO

Numbers in random order? YES

AB Pattern? NO

ABC Pattern? Yes

Answer = 8

10

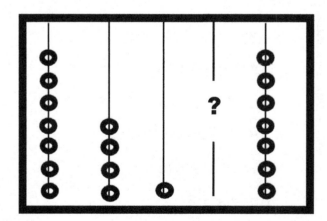

Numbers Going Up? NO

Numbers Going Down? Yes

Use Counting Down Then Up Pattern

Answer = 4

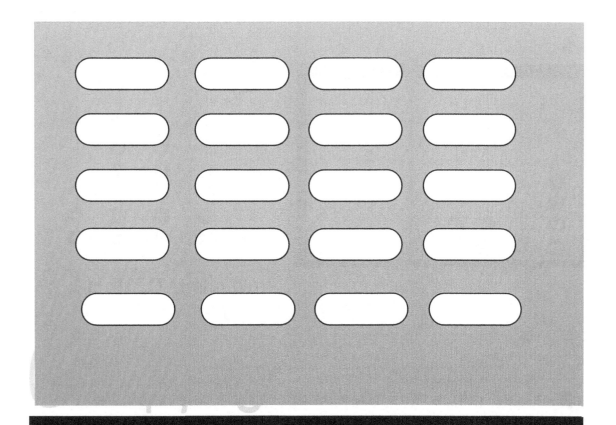

PRACTICE TEST

1

2

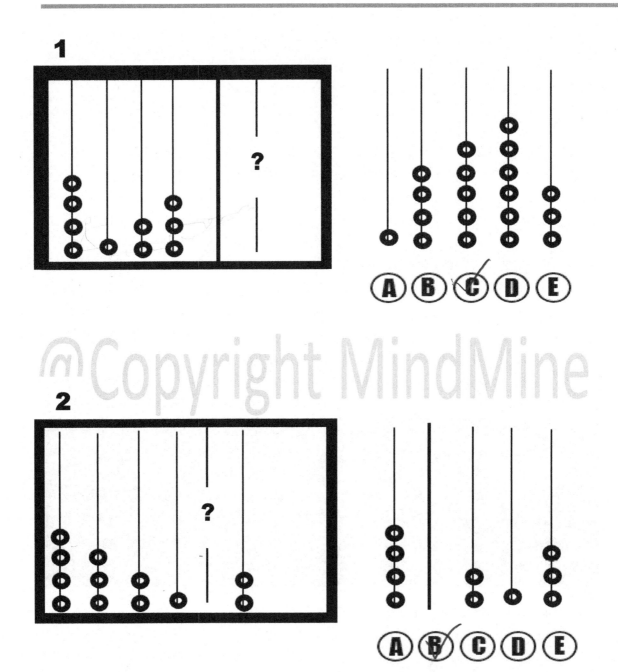

3

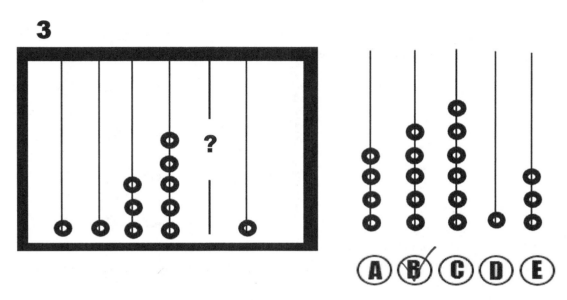

4

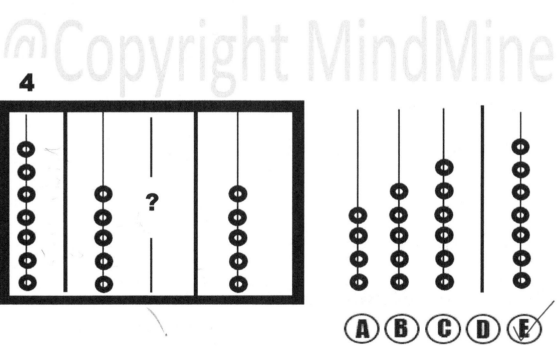

5

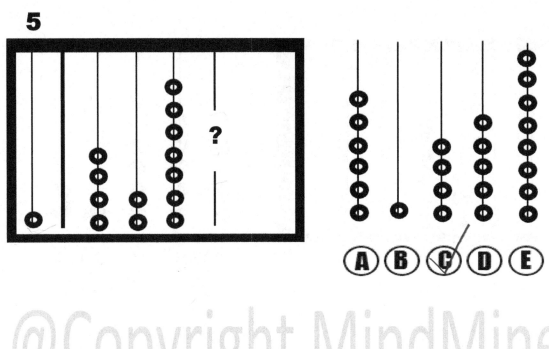

6

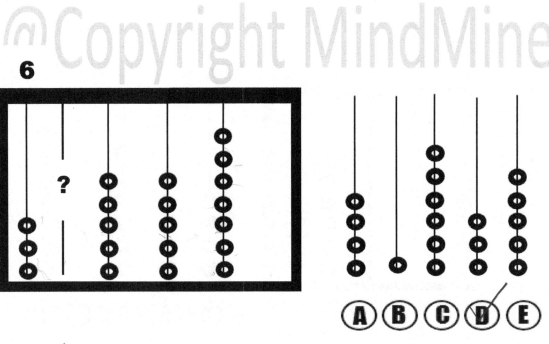

7

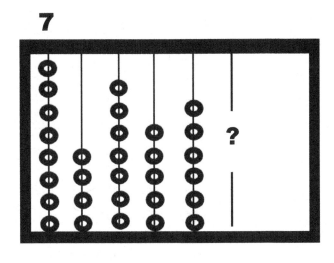

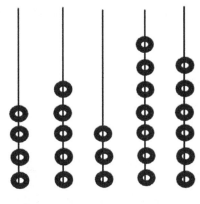

A **B** **C** **D** **E**

8

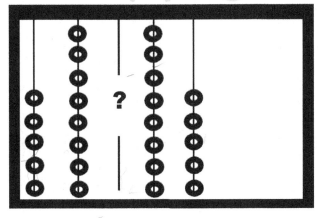

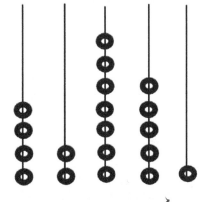

A **B** **C** **D** **E**

9

10

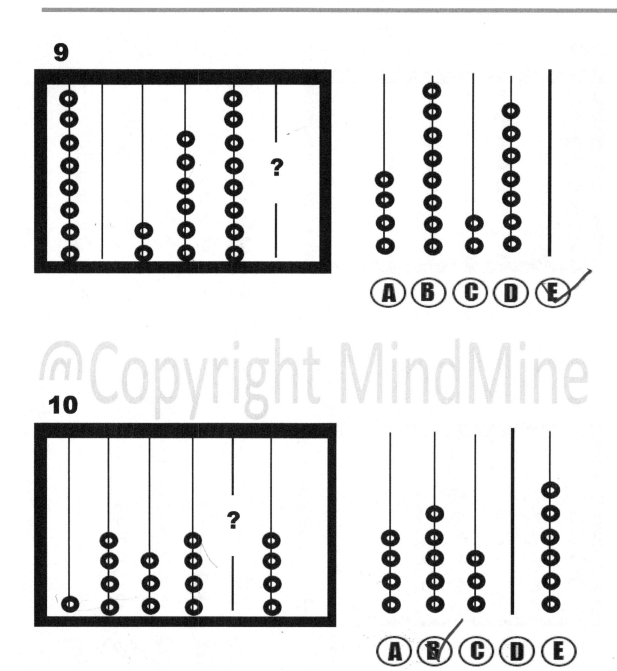

11

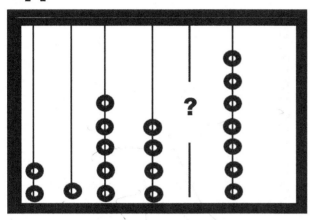

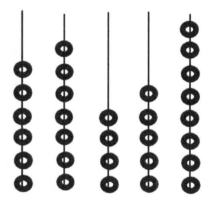

(A) (B) (C) (D) (E)

12

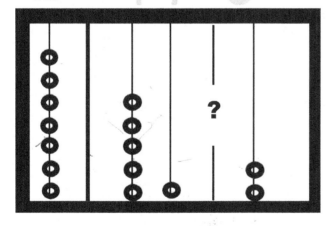

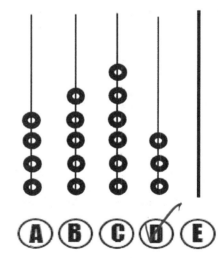

(A) (B) (C) (D) (E)

13

14

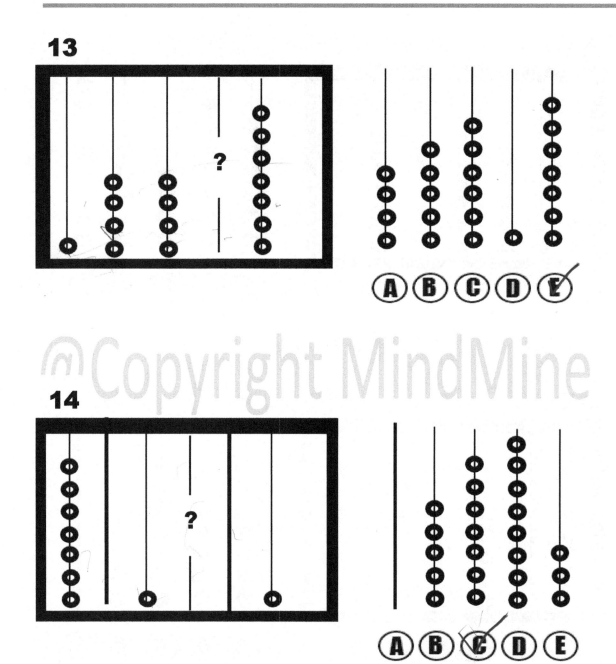

15

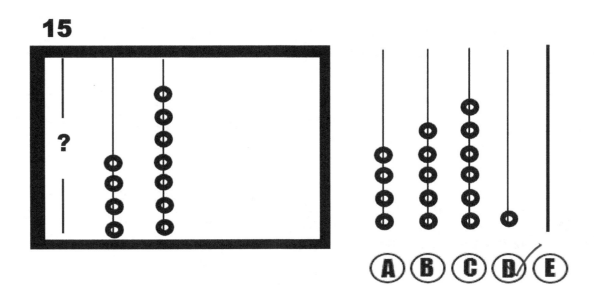

16

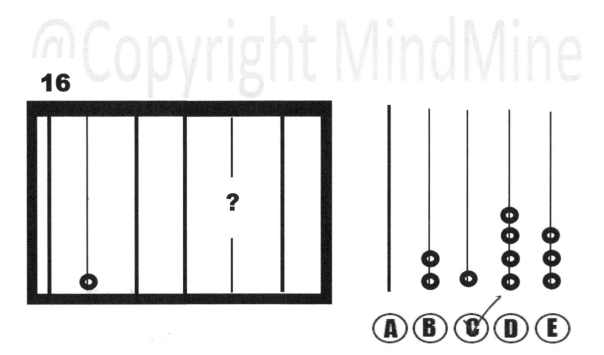

17

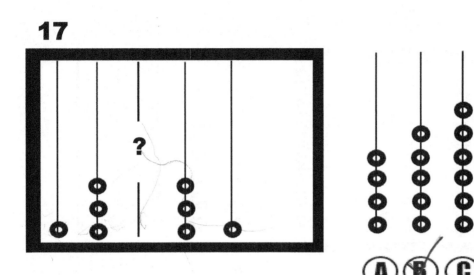

18

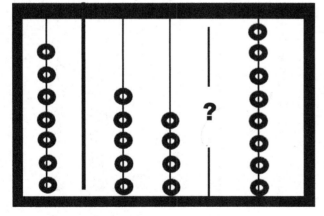

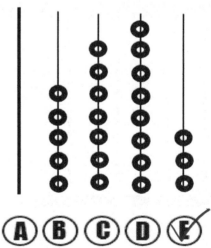

19

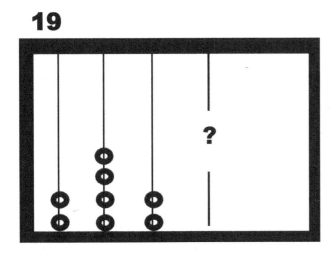
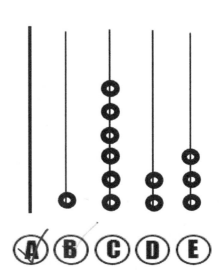

20

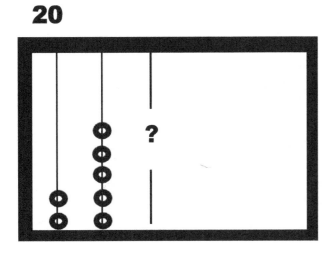
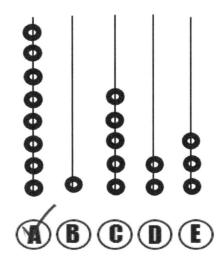

1. Ⓐ Ⓑ Ⓒ Ⓓ Ⓔ
2. Ⓐ Ⓑ Ⓒ Ⓓ Ⓔ
3. Ⓐ Ⓑ Ⓒ Ⓓ Ⓔ
4. Ⓐ Ⓑ Ⓒ Ⓓ Ⓔ
5. Ⓐ Ⓑ Ⓒ Ⓓ Ⓔ
6. Ⓐ Ⓑ Ⓒ Ⓓ Ⓔ
7. Ⓐ Ⓑ Ⓒ Ⓓ Ⓔ
8. Ⓐ Ⓑ Ⓒ Ⓓ Ⓔ
9. Ⓐ Ⓑ Ⓒ Ⓓ Ⓔ
10. Ⓐ Ⓑ Ⓒ Ⓓ Ⓔ
11. Ⓐ Ⓑ Ⓒ Ⓓ Ⓔ
12. Ⓐ Ⓑ Ⓒ Ⓓ Ⓔ
13. Ⓐ Ⓑ Ⓒ Ⓓ Ⓔ
14. Ⓐ Ⓑ Ⓒ Ⓓ Ⓔ
15. Ⓐ Ⓑ Ⓒ Ⓓ Ⓔ
16. Ⓐ Ⓑ Ⓒ Ⓓ Ⓔ
17. Ⓐ Ⓑ Ⓒ Ⓓ Ⓔ
18. Ⓐ Ⓑ Ⓒ Ⓓ Ⓔ
19. Ⓐ Ⓑ Ⓒ Ⓓ Ⓔ
20. Ⓐ Ⓑ Ⓒ Ⓓ Ⓔ

ANSWERS

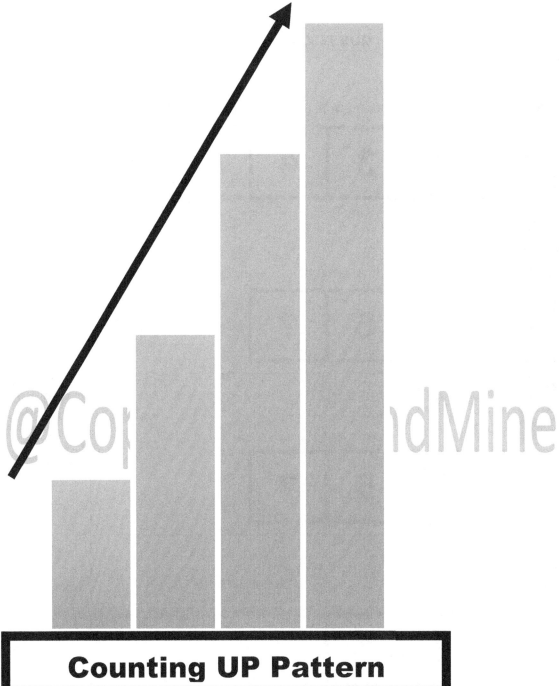

Counting UP Pattern

QUESTION	ANSWER
1 +1 +1 +1 +1 +1 1 2 3 4 5 ?	D
2 +2 +2 +2 2 4 6 ?	A
3 +2 +2 +2 1 3 5 ?	D
4 +3 +3 0 3 ?	C
5 +4 +4 0 4 ?	A

6   C

+3   +3

| 1 | 4 | ? |

7   C

+2   +2

| 0 | 2 | ? |

8   E

+3   +3

| ? | 3 | 6 |

9   A

+2   +2   +2

| ? | 3 | 5 | 7 |

10   B

+1   +1   +1

| 4 | 5 | 6 | ? |

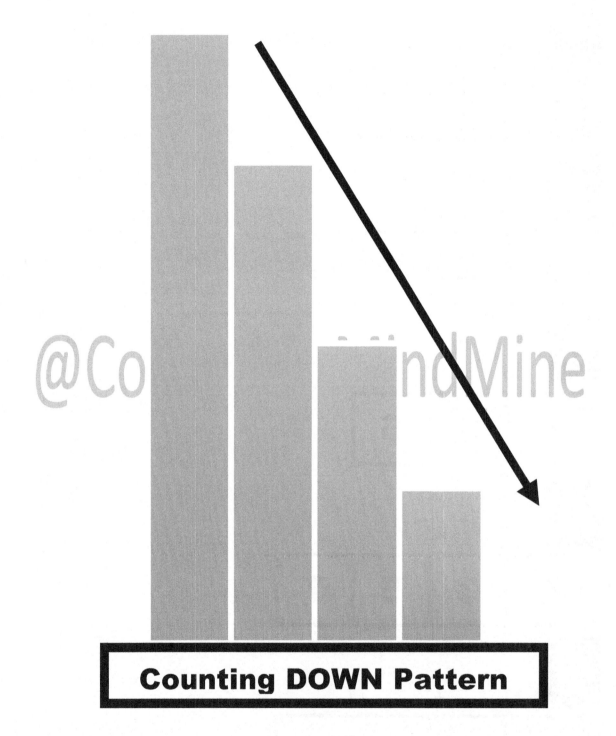

Counting DOWN Pattern

NUMBER SERIES – Counting DOWN Pattern

QUESTION	ANSWER
1 ~1 ~1 ~1 ~1 ~1 7 6 5 4 3 ?	E
2 ~2 ~2 ~2 8 6 4 ?	B
3 ~2 ~2 ~2 7 5 3 ?	D
4 ~4 ~4 8 4 ?	B
5 ~3 ~3 6 3 ?	E

MindMine

NUMBER SERIES – Counting DOWN Pattern

6 | A

~2 ~2 ~2

| 6 | 4 | 2 | ? |

7 | C

~3 ~3

| 7 | 4 | ? |

8 | A

~3 ~3

| 8 | 5 | ? |

9 | A

~1 ~1 ~1

| 3 | 2 | 1 | ? |

10 | A

~2 ~2 ~2

| 7 | ? | 3 | 1 |

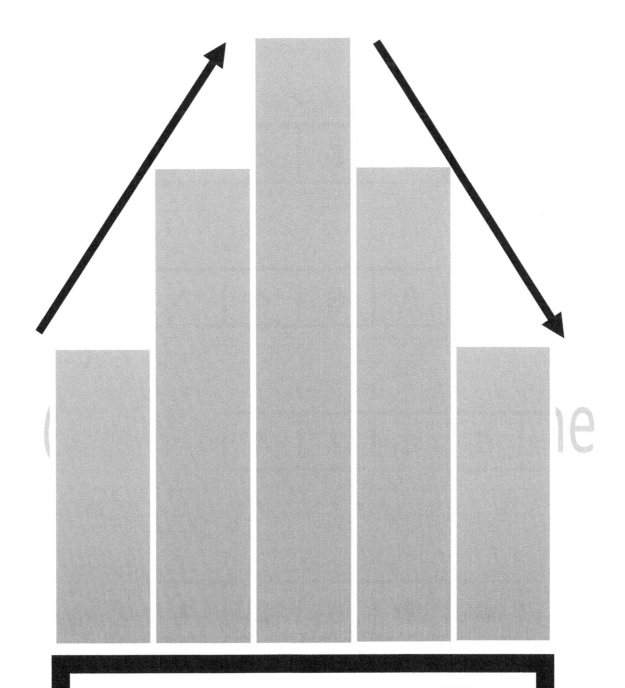

Counting UP then DOWN Pattern

QUESTION	ANSWER
1 +2 +2 -2 -2 -2 3 | 5 | 7 | 5 | 3 | ?	**C**
2 +2 +2 -2 -2 -2 4 | 6 | 8 | 6 | 4 | ?	**B**
3 +1 +1 -1 -1 4 | 5 | 6 | ? | 4	**A**
4 +2 +2 +2 -2 -2 2 | 4 | ? | 8 | 6 | 4	**D**
5 +3 +3 -3 -3 2 | 5 | 8 | ? | 2	**E**

NUMBER SERIES – Counting UP then DOWN Pattern

QUESTION	ANSWER
6 +3 +3 -3 -3 ? 4 7 4 1	**E**
7 +2 +2 +2 -2 1 ? 5 7 5	**B**
8 +3 +3 -3 2 5 ? 5	**E**
9 +2 +2 +0 -2 -2 1 3 5 5 3 ?	**B**
10 +2 +2 +0 -2 -2 2 4 6 6 4 ?	**B**

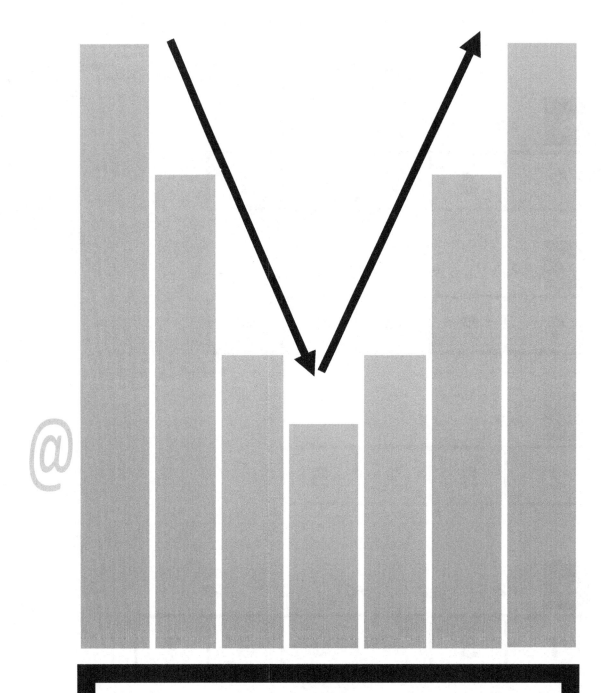

Counting DOWN then UP Pattern

NUMBER SERIES – Counting DOWN then UP Pattern

QUESTION	ANSWER
1 -1 -1 -1 +1 +1 7 | 6 | 5 | 4 | 5 | ?	**D**
2 -2 -2 +2 +2 8 | 6 | 4 | ? | 8	**B**
3 -3 -3 +3 +3 8 | 5 | ? | 5 | 8	**B**
4 -2 +0 +2 7 | 5 | ? | 7	**C**
5 -4 +0 +4 8 | 4 | ? | 8	**A**

QUESTION	ANSWER
6 -3 -3 +3 | ? | 5 | 2 | 5 |	**E**
7 -3 -3 +3 +3 | 7 | 4 | 1 | ? | 7 |	**A**
8 -4 +4 +4 | 4 | 0 | 4 | ? |	**E**
9 -2 -2 +0 +2 +2 | 5 | 3 | 1 | 1 | ? | 5 |	**E**
10 -4 -4 +0 +4 +4 | 8 | 4 | 0 | ? | 4 | 8 |	**B**

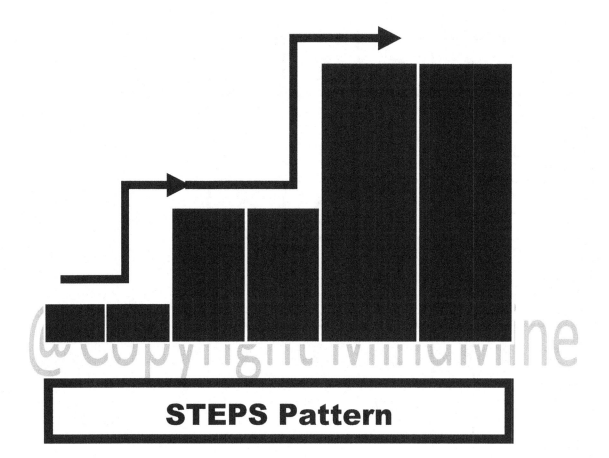

STEPS Pattern

QUESTION	ANSWER

1   +0   +1   +0   +1   +0

1	1	2	2	3	?

D

---

2   +0   +3   +0   +3

3	3	6	?	9

D

---

3   +0   -2   +0   -2

5	?	3	3	1

C

---

4   +0   +3   +0

3	?	6	6

E

---

5   -2   +0   -2   +0

6	4	4	?	2

E

QUESTION	ANSWER
6 +2 +0 +2 +0 0 | 2 | 2 | 4 | ?	**A**
7 +0 +3 +0 +3 +0 1 | 1 | 4 | 4 | ? | 7	**B**
8 +0 -3 +0 -3 8 | ? | 5 | 5 | 2	**E**
9 +0 +2 +0 -2 +0 3 | 3 | 5 | 5 | 3 | ?	**E**
10 +0 -4 +0 -4 8 | 8 | 4 | ? | 0	**A**

AB Pattern

NUMBER SERIES – **AB Pattern**

QUESTION	ANSWER
1 *+3* *-3* *+3* 1 4 1 ?	**A**
2 *+4* *-4* *+4* 2 6 ? 6	**E**
3 *-4* *+4* *-4* 5 1 ? 1	**B**
4 *+3* *-3* *+3* 4 7 4 ?	**D**
5 *+3* *-3* *+3* 1 4 1 ?	**A**
6 *+4* *-4* *+4* ? 6 2 6	**C**

QUESTION	ANSWER
7 *-7* *+7* *-7* ? | 1 | 8 | 1	E
8 *+3* *-3* *+3* 4 | ? | 4 | 7	D
9 *-4* *+4* *-4* 6 | 2 | ? | 2	C
10 *+6* *-6* *+6* 1 | 7 | 1 | ?	D
11 *-2* *+2* *-2* 2 | 0 | ? | 0	E
12 *+4* *-4* *+4* 0 | 4 | ? | 4	C

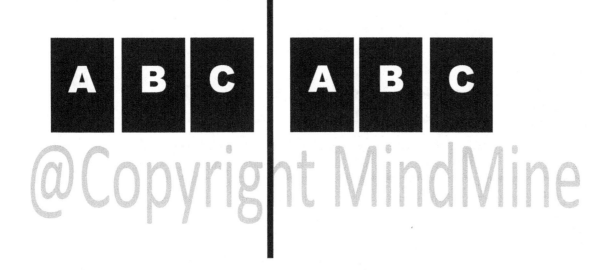

ABC Pattern

NUMBER SERIES – **ABC Pattern**

QUESTION	ANSWER
1 *+3* *+2* *-5* *+3* *+2* 1 | 4 | 6 | 1 | 4 | ?	**C**
2 *-2* *+5* *-3* *-2* *+5* 4 | 2 | 7 | 4 | ? | 7	**B**
3 *-4* *+0* *+4* *-4* *+0* 5 | 1 | 1 | 5 | ? | 1	**B**
4 *+4* *-1* *-3* *+4* *-1* ? | 8 | 7 | 4 | 8 | 7	**E**
5 *-7* *-1* *+8* *-7* *-1* 8 | 1 | 0 | 8 | ? | 0	**B**
6 *+4* *-6* *+2* *+4* *-6* ? | 6 | 0 | 2 | 6 | 0	**C**

QUESTION	ANSWER
7 -2 +7 -5 -2 +7 3 | 1 | 8 | 3 | 1 | ?	D
8 -1 +4 -3 -1 +4 4 | ? | 7 | 4 | 3 | 7	B
9 +3 -4 +1 +3 -4 ? | 6 | 2 | 3 | 6 | 2	A
10 +6 -4 -2 +6 -4 1 | 7 | 3 | 1 | ? | 3	D
11 +3 -5 +2 +3 -5 2 | 5 | 0 | 2 | 5 | ?	E
12 +4 +3 -7 +4 +3 0 | 4 | 7 | 0 | 4 | ?	A

ABCD Pattern

NUMBER SERIES – **ABCD Pattern**

QUESTION	ANSWER
1 5 1 4 8 | 5 1 4 ?	E
2 4 2 7 1 | ? 2 7	A
3 8 ? 5 4 | 8 1 5 4	D
4 ? 0 4 8 | 3 0 4 8	B
5 5 8 1 0 | 5 8 1 ?	E
6 ? 6 3 1 | 0 6 3	B

QUESTION	ANSWER
7 1 5 3 8 | 1 ? 3 8	B
8 4 ? 7 3 | 4 0 7	C
9 0 3 5 ? | 0 3 5 2	D
10 1 7 3 4 | 1 ? 3	E
11 8 2 5 ? | 8 2 5 1	D
12 ? 0 4 7 | 1 0 4 7	A

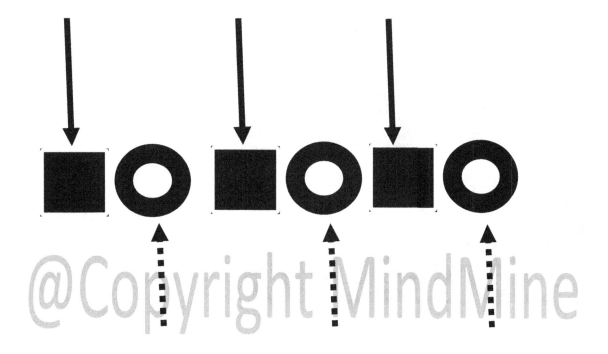

SKIP Pattern

QUESTION	ANSWER
1 1 8 3 7 5 ?	**D**
2 7 1 5 3 3 ?	**B**
3 8 2 6 ? 4 6	**A**
4 7 0 5 ? 3 0	**E**
5 1 0 4 2 7 ?	**A**

NUMBER SERIES – SKIP Pattern

QUESTION	ANSWER
6 1 3 3 3 5 ? 7	D
7 8 1 7 2 6 ?	C
8 4 ? 4 3 4 5	E
9 8 0 6 2 4 ?	A
10 1 8 3 8 ? 8	B

@copyright MindMine

QUESTION	ANSWER
11 2 1 4 4 ? 8	**A**
12 7 0 ? 1 3 2	**B**
13 1 2 1 4 ? 6	**D**
14 7 0 ? 1 7 2	**C**
15 2 6 4 4 ? 2	**C**

© copyright MindMine

NUMBER SERIES – SKIP Pattern

QUESTION	ANSWER
16 0 ? 1 5 2 7	E
17 8 2 6 1 4 ?	D
18 5 ? 6 0 7 0	B
19 2 8 4 7 6 ?	C
20 5 0 4 ? 3 2	D

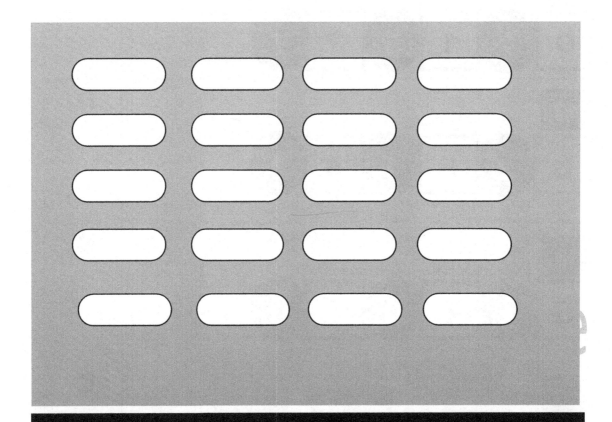

PRACTICE TEST

QUESTION	ANSWER	PATTERN
1	C	SKIP
2	D	Count Down-Stay-Up
3	D	ABCD
4	E	ABC
5	C	SKIP
6	D	STEPS
7	E	STEPS
8	D	AB
9	E	ABCD
10	B	SKIP
11	E	SKIP
12	D	SKIP
13	E	STEPS
14	C	ABC
15	D	Count Up
16	C	ABC
17	B	Count Up then Down
18	E	SKIP
19	A	Count Up then Down
20	A	Count Up

Made in the USA
Coppell, TX
09 September 2020